HISTORY OF
ROYAL BLUE EXPRESS SERVICES

GW00578187

OTHER BOOKS BY THE SAME AUTHORS

R. C. Anderson

History of the Tramways of Bournemouth and Poole
Great Orme Railway
History of the Llandudno and Colwyn Bay Electric Railway
  Limited
History of the Tramways of East Anglia

G. Frankis

Rambles Around Exeter
with J. R. Yonge
Transport in the Grand Duchy of Luxembourg

Royal Blue coach en route

HISTORY
OF ROYAL BLUE
EXPRESS SERVICES

by

R. C. ANDERSON, AM Inst T and G. FRANKIS

DAVID & CHARLES : NEWTON ABBOT

7153 4734 9

COPYRIGHT NOTICE
© R. C. ANDERSON AND G. FRANKIS 1970
All Rights Reserved. No part of this publication may be reproduced, stored in a retrieval system, or transmitted, in any form or by any means, electronic, mechanical, photocopying, recording or otherwise, without the prior permission of David & Charles (Publishers) Limited

Note : Decimal equivalents are given in brackets after amounts of money from 6d to £1, eg £3 10s 6d (£3.53) and 12s 10d (64p) The information in this book represents the position at 31 August 1969

Printed in Great Britain by
Bristol Typesetting Company Limited
Barton Manor St Philips Bristol
and set in eleven on thirteen point Baskerville
for David & Charles (Publishers) Ltd
South Devon House Newton Abbot Devon

CONTENTS

LIST OF ILLUSTRATIONS

PLATES

MAPS

LINE ILLUSTRATIONS

ACKNOWLEDGMENTS

The authors gratefully acknowledge the help given to them in the preparation of the manuscript by H. L. Ellis, FCA, M Inst T, Director & General Manager of the Western & Southern National Omnibus Companies; L. T. Duncan, Traffic Manager of the Western & Southern National Omnibus Companies; H. H. Elliott, the last survivor of the three Elliott Bros who founded the Royal Blue Express Coach business; and C. H. Preece, M Inst T, Traffic Manager for Elliott Bros and later Traffic Manager (Commercial) of the Western/Southern National Omnibus Cos. Thanks must also be recorded to S. C. Bullock, founder and director of Tourist Motor Coaches (Southampton) Ltd, for information regarding his company; to R. J. Crawley for his assistance with the fleet detail; and to J. R. Yonge, who kindly drew the maps.

The authors are also indebted to J. Gleeson, Traffic Superintendent, Royal Blue Express Services, Bournemouth and to S. W. Tucker, Traffic Assistant (Express Services) of the Western/Southern National Omnibus Cos, who read the text and suggested several helpful additions and alterations.

With regard to the photographs, those reproduced in the frontispiece and on pages 53 (top), 54 (both), 71 (right), 72 (both), 90 (middle and bottom), 107 (all three), 108 (all three), 125 (top and bottom), and all those on 126, 143, and 144 are from the official records of the Western/Southern National Omnibus Companies; and those on pages 17 (both), 18, 35, 36 (middle and bottom), and 89 (both) are from the personal collection of Mr H. H. Elliott. Photographs on pages 36 (top), 53 (bottom), 90 (top) and 125 (middle) were kindly lent by Bournemouth Corporation Transport Department, Duple Motor Bodies Limited, C. E. Pounds Esq, and R. A. Pryor Esq.

FOREWORD

As the last surviving son of the late Mr Thomas Elliott, Founder of the 'Royal Blue' in 1880, with vivid memories from childhood through the horse days and the whole progress of this story, I consider it a pleasure and privilege to assist in recording the continued advancement, keen effort and foresight put into this now 'National Enterprise' and to congratulate the present organisation, management and staff.

H. H. ELLIOTT, 1968

INTRODUCTION

ON a busy Saturday in summer if you happen to go to London's Victoria Coach Station, or indeed to any one of the coach or bus stations throughout Britain, you will be presented with a living gazetteer of the country as the coaches stream out showing destinations as far afield as Cardiff, Edinburgh, Norwich, Penzance, and a thousand points between.

The huge development which has resulted in the rebirth of the stage coaches of the eighteenth and nineteenth centuries under their present name of 'Long Distance Express Services' is a romance of modern development and science which deserves more appreciation than in fact it has received. The story, of course, is not just one of achievement by the coach operators themselves. The road engineer, the vehicle builder, the tyre manufacturers, and indeed almost every modern industry, have contributed to the provision of the wonderful vehicles and network of services which run week in and week out over the length and breadth of this country.

Apart from the very great range of this development, one must marvel at the speed at which it has been achieved. The motor vehicle came into use only at the very end of the nineteenth century but by 1950 the picture of the services was virtually complete.

It seems very doubtful whether in fact there was a complete break between the mail coaches of the eighteenth/nineteenth centuries and the rebirth of modern coach services. It is, of course, beyond doubt that the invention of the locomotive engine and the development of the railways virtually killed the mail coach services. As each new rail route opened, so the passengers quickly deserted the slow horse-drawn service. Hotels and inns fell into disuse and decay and neglect spread to the roads where previously all had been colour and life.

In remote parts of the country however, the horse-drawn coaches continued as feeders to the nearest railhead. Even today, you may find vehicles preserved bearing route indications such as Minehead–Lynton or Bideford–Clovelly, both covering sections of country never invaded by the railways.

The railways themselves introduced feeder services in Cornwall as early as 1903, so that it requires no great stretch of imagination to feel certain that in fact somewhere the 'mail' services lived on in the remote parts of the country and bridged the gap between the pre-rail and present road periods.

Charles Dickens was the great chronicler of the horse-drawn days, with his vivid descriptions of journeys across the length and breadth of the country. Unfortunately, no such writer or historian has recorded the modern scene. Perhaps the ubiquity and mechanical certainty of the modern vehicle has killed the romance.

In the following pages the authors tell the story of Royal Blue Express Services, one of the largest networks in this particular field. One seeks in a story of this kind to avoid long lists of statistics and dates, but to give some idea of the extent of the development and the size of the operations today the following figures should prove of interest :

Royal Blue Express Services
1936 Total Annual Revenue £ 103,500
1968 ,, ,, ,, £1,000,000

During the course of the story, we shall read a good deal about Associated Motorways. This organisation is, in fact, a partnership of limited companies formed in the early 1930s. It came into being following the 1930 Road Traffic Act and as a result of the welter of applications and cross applications concerning services already being provided over common routes by the competing interests.

Royal Blue became a very active member of the organisation

and have remained so to the present day. The total revenue earned by Associated Motorways and Royal Blue together amounts to £2,400,000 per annum.

The eighty-five years covered by this story of Royal Blue are also the years during which the 'Motor Age' has come, if not to final maturity, at least a very long way from the first 'phut-phut' of the Daimler Benz and other pioneer 'horseless carriages'.

C. H. PREECE

Branksome Mews, 1880, the birthplace of Royal Blue

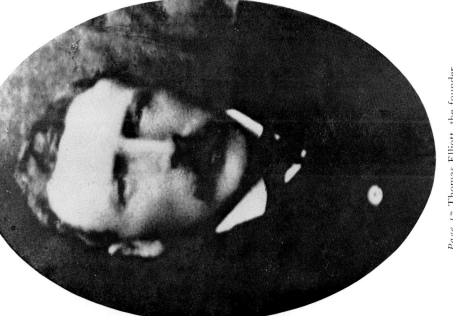

Page 17 Thomas Elliott, the founder

Page 18 Decorated horse-drawn coach

CHAPTER ONE

THE FAMILY BUSINESS 1880-1918

COACHING IN THE WEST COUNTRY

BEFORE considering how Elliott's Royal Blue services
came into existence, it is perhaps worthwhile looking at
the general background. It is not possible to draw a
definite line and say, 'Express Services by road for the conveyance of passengers started on such and such a date'. Like most
things, they were part of a continuous evolution, and to set the
scene, it is proposed to describe briefly the development of coaching and how the coming of the railways changed the pattern.

There is a direct link between the original mail coaches of the
seventeenth/nineteenth centuries (even these coaches have their
predecessors in history) and the present network of bus and coach
services. The original heavy, lumbering, vehicles, which conveyed separate passengers and goods for hire and reward, were
supplemented by coaches let out for hire—in fact 'hackney'
coaches—a development which led to stage coaches and to the
famous mail coaches. Among the first stage coaches in the West
Country was the one which operated between Exeter and Falmouth and connected with the famous 'Falmouth Packet' Boats.
The journey took two days and when, in 1790, the service was
extended to London, the through journey took five days; fares
were based on a rate of 6d (2.5p) per mile inside and 4d per
mile outside. It will be seen that the rates charged were very
much higher than those of today and this meant that the stage
and mail coaches were the mode of travel for richer people;
the poorer had to be content with lumbering canvas-covered
carts, known as stage-wagons.

In August 1784, the first mail coach service was introduced; this operated between Bristol and London, a route later to be worked by Royal Blue motor coaches. Development of similar services was rapid and in 1799 a mail coach began operating between Falmouth and Exeter, taking a day on the journey. Subsequently, the service was extended to London and by 1835 fierce competition had reduced the running time between London and Falmouth to 35 hours. This high speed run was accomplished by the 'Royal Quicksilver Mail', and one of the actual coaches has been preserved in the Hull Transport Museum. It was the fastest provincial coach out of London and, with twenty changes of horses, accomplished the 176 miles between London and Exeter in $17\frac{1}{2}$ hours.

By 1836 there were some 700 of these light mail coaches and about 3,000 stage coaches, which together provided a network of regular services throughout England. 'England' is mentioned intentionally, as the stage and mail coaches were almost unknown in Scotland and Wales. These coaches operated to a regular timetable and the overall average speed was about 10 mph.

Further east, the first regular coach service into Dorset was thought to have been introduced between Weymouth and London to coincide with visits to Weymouth by King George III. The Weymouth–London service operated daily except Sundays, and the 'Magnet' coach departed from outside Lucas Hotel (the present Victoria Hotel) Weymouth at 4.45 am, arriving in Piccadilly the same evening at 8 o'clock—a journey of $15\frac{1}{4}$ hours. By 1824 services were so arranged that it was also possible to connect at Dorchester with a stage or mail coach to or from Exeter. The opening of the Liverpool and Manchester Railway in 1830 was an event of great significance for both coach travel and the development of land transport throughout the world. The impact of the railways on coaches was such that by the early 1840s the majority of coach proprietors realised they were faced with ruin. There was much unemployment among the large number of persons engaged in operating the network of coach services and this in turn drove coaching inns out of business. At the same time the roads became comparatively deserted and gradually fell into decay. Indeed, for the next forty years, Britain's highways were forgotten and the Red Flag Act of 1865 did not help matters, as it required an attendant with a red flag to walk in front of all mechanically propelled road vehicles. Although the red flag was abolished in 1878 by the Highways & Locomotives Amendment Act, it was still compulsory for an attendant to walk 20 yd in front of a vehicle. The practice was finally discontinued for cars and locomotives under 3 tons weight by Acts of 1896 and 1898 but heavier vehicles were not exempted until 1904.

However, in the West Country the impact of railways was not felt so rapidly and mail and stage coaches continued to operate on a number of routes. Hampshire was linked with Dorset by a service on three days a week between Weymouth and Southampton. This alternated on three other days per week with a Southampton–Bristol service and, in addition, coaches operated from such places as Taunton and Poole, the whole providing a network of services throughout the west not unlike the present pattern of Royal Blue Services.

THE DEVELOPMENT OF BOURNEMOUTH

It was only in the latter half of the nineteenth century that modern Bournemouth began to develop as a desirable place in which to live or spend one's holidays. By 1881 the population was about 17,000 persons and in 1883 the town was incorporated as a borough.

Local public transport was provided by services of horse-drawn buses, the first having started in 1872 between Southbourne and Bournemouth at a return fare of one shilling (5p). Evidence of the rapid development of the area came in 1881 when the Bournemouth, Poole and District Light Railway (Electric) Co proposed the construction of a 6 mile tramway from Bournemouth East (now Central) Station to Poole, but they were unable to obtain the necessary powers.

Other horse-bus operators began to operate, including the

Bournemouth, Boscombe and Westbourne Omnibus Co, who operated a thirty minute service between County Gates and Boscombe, from 1889. Further developments in local transport came when the Poole and District Electric Traction Co opened a line from County Gates to Poole Railway Station on 6 April 1901. Bournemouth Corporation introduced its own scheme of tramways, the first section running from the Lansdowne to Pokesdown (Warwick Road) on 23 July 1902. Other sections were opened soon afterwards and the purchase of the Poole and District Electric Traction Co resulted in a through service opening on 3 July 1905 between Poole and Bournemouth, with a subsequent extension to Christchurch. With the introduction of the tramways, the horse-bus operators disappeared from the streets of Bournemouth.

It is not, perhaps, surprising that the area did not prove an immediate attraction to the early promoters of railways, although by means of a branch line from the Ringwood Junction Railway Station of the 'Southampton & Dorchester Railway', it was possible to reach Christchurch by rail in 1862 and Bournemouth itself by 1870. In the latter year, the 'Square' was laid out, in place of a narrow wooden bridge across the Bourne stream.

The town was growing rapidly and there was a need for an alternative method of linking Bournemouth with the railway.

ELLIOTT'S ROYAL BLUE

As so often happens in any story of human achievement, chance took a hand in the establishment of Elliott's Royal Blue. In this case the motivating factor was the indirect railway route to Bournemouth, and it would seem that Mr Thomas Elliott took advantage of the situation by establishing a short road link over the route of the present main road into Christchurch and Bournemouth.

Thomas Elliott had from an early age been associated with the coach and jobmaster's business and was only 22 years old when he founded 'Royal Blue and Branksome Mews' in 1880 at Avenue Lane, Avenue Road, Bournemouth. At this time Tom

Elliott (as he was popularly known) was living in a cottage in Commercial Road, Bournemouth, backing on to Avenue Lane. The present 'Marks & Spencer' store stands upon the site. Thomas Elliott's business cards of this period describe him as 'Job Master & Carriage Builder'.

The cottage became part of 'Branksome Mews' and a large glass-covered yard on the right-hand side of Avenue Lane housed the stables, loose boxes, and coach houses. On the left-hand side of the 'Lane' were the offices and premises, illuminated by gas lighting during hours of darkness. On each side of the 'Lane' were hay, straw, and corn lofts with shutes into the food store and stables. Manure containers stood at the far end of the yard and baskets were kept behind all the horses. Straw-plaited mats were kept everywhere, for the visiting gentry to walk upon when inspecting and selecting the horses, hacks, and hunters they might wish to hire.

Elliotts were coach builders, repairers and painters, saddlers, harness makers, and blacksmiths. A large Crossley gas engine drove the chaff cutters, oat rollers, bean and maize crushers and it was the duty of one man and his son to service these machines and attend to the cutting and crushing of the various foodstuffs. They lived in the lofts above. Hay, straw, and corn were delivered direct from Hampshire and Dorset farms by wagons, mostly travelling at night, each drawn by three shire horses.

As the business developed, Mr Elliott kept every class of horse-drawn vehicle—four-in-hand coaches, four large char-a-bancs, buses, landaus, broughams, victorias, dog carts, governess carts, double chairs, rally carts, two and four wheeled phaetons, wagonettes, etc—all of which were available for hire.

In addition to vehicles, Mr Elliott kept a large stud of good, useful, and reliable horses, including several well matched pairs, ladies' and gentlemen's hacks, and hunters. Special horses and ponies were kept for patrons to drive themselves in the various types of vehicles for hire. Both horses and vehicles were kept in splendid condition and a contemporary account states that 'they were turned out in a style to do credit to any private establishment of any gentleman, whilst the coachmen and drivers were notable for their punctuality and polite attention'.

It is not surprising that Mr Elliott's venture was successful and that he secured the confidence and support of a very extensive and high class patronage. Mr Elliott became well-known and highly respected in Bournemouth and was employed to bring the first Charter of Incorporation granted to Bournemouth, which arrived in the Borough on 28 August 1883.

Yet another branch of the business during the horse era was the large covered Riding School in Oxford Road. Here, well lit by gas lighting, with a balcony all round from which parents and friends could watch the children and others learning horsemanship, was a riding ring. Its floor was composed of deep peat and jumps of all types and sizes were available.

The riding master was an ex-army major, who always arrived in immaculate attire—breeches, boots, hacking jacket, stock, and bowler hat. His usual habit after doffing his hat to the assembled company was to chat with them, then mount and ride away with his pupils. To the staff he was always 'Sir', to the pupils, 'Major' or 'Mr'. At that time, of course, all the ladies and girls rode side-saddle, attired in their riding habits. Lessons were also given in four-in-hand or tandem driving.

Subsequently, Tom Elliott was joined in his business by his three sons, Jack, Harry, and Ted. The three boys delivered the first *Bournemouth Daily Echo* by pony and trap, provided transport for town hall officials and were the youngest four-in-hand drivers licensed to carry passengers. One gathers that a high degree of efficiency and hard work was required by their father and some measure of this can be seen from the fact that in 1899 H. H. (Harry) Elliott, then aged 8 years, won a show jumping cup against riders of all ages.

But to return to the rail feeder service. This was operated by four-in-hand stage coaches and connected with the 'Southampton & Dorchester Railway' at Holmsley Station in the New Forest. So far as records exist, the service is believed to have started in 1880 and its route passed the 'Cat & Fiddle' inn on the Bournemouth–Lyndhurst road. A change of horses took place at the

FIRST PRIZE COACHES.

First Prize, Aug. 20th, 1896 ; First Prize and Champion Banner, Aug. 19th, 1897 ; First
Prize, Aug. 1899 ; First Prize, May, 1900 ; also 2nd Prize with **Landau and Four Horse**
Postillion, 1901.

TELEPHONE No. 262.

ELLIOTT'S "ROYAL BLUE"
COACHES and CHARS-A-BANC

WILL RUN TO THE FOLLOWING PLACES OF INTEREST EVERY DAY—

LYMINGTON & MILFORD-ON-SEA every Thursday at 10.30.

Passing by Newlands Manor, Highcliff Castle, with a beautiful drive of eight miles
by the Solent, a most picturesque drive ..   .. **FARE 6/-**

WIMBORNE and CANFORD PARK at 2.45.

Seat of Lord Wimborne, Passing through the Model Village of Canford. Returning
by way of Broadstone, the Old Roman Road, Tichborne Estate, Parkstone, giving splendid
views of the Purbeck Hills, Branksea Island, Corfe Castle, and the Poole New Park, through
the Penn Hill Estate and Branksome Park   ..   .. **FARE 3/-**

HAVEN HOTEL and SANDBANKS at 10.45 and 2.45.

The route taken is via the New West Cliff Drive, passing Durley, Middle, and Alum
Chine through the Branksome Woods, passing by Shell Bay and round Poole Harbour to
the Haven Hotel. Returning via Canford Cliffs and Branksome Chine and the Rhododendron
Avenue, Branksome Park. Visitors to Bournemouth should not miss this Drive, as it is
the finest Short Drive in the South of England.   ..   ..   .. **FARE 2/-**

HERON COURT & RHODODENDRON FOREST at 10.45 & 2.45

The seat of the Earl of Malmesbury.
The route taken is via East Cliff Drive, King's Park, over the Iford Bridge, through
the Oak Avenue, passing by the Blackwater Ferry and returning via Littledown, Queen's
Park and Richmond Park   ..   .. **FARE 2/-**

BRANKSOME CHINE & CANFORD CLIFFS at 10.45 & 2.45

Circular tour of nearly 10 miles through the picturesque roads of Branksome Park
and Canford Cliffs. Time is allowed for a walk through the Chine ..   .. **FARE 1/-**

STOUR VALLEY, HOLDENHURST & THROOP at 10.45 & 2.45

Circular Tour of about 10 miles. The route taken is via Dean Park and Charminster
Road, through Queen's Park (Golf Links), passing " Littledown," the seat of J. E. Cooper-
Dean, Esq., J.P., and through Holdenhurst Village (by the " Mother Church " of Bourne-
mouth) then to the Stour Ford, Throop, returning by way of Muscliff, Redhill, Moordown,
Winton and Meyrick Park (Golf Links) ..   .. **FARE 1/-**

GORDON WOOD & SOUTHBOURNE at 10.45 & 2.45. Fare 1/-

Orders received for Landaus, Wagonettes and Cabs to and from the Stations, and every des-
cription of Carriages at Reasonable Prices. Horses taken in at Livery. Lessons given
in Tandem or Four-in-Hand Driving by ELLIOTT BROS.
Booking Offices—STOUR VALE DAIRY, The Square ; PARSONS' DAIRY, BOS-
COMBE ; and ROYAL BLUE MEWS, Avenue Lane ;
WHERE SEATS CAN BE BOOKED IN ADVANCE.

Proprietors : ELLIOTT BROS., BOURNEMOUTH.

N.B.—Messrs. ELLIOTT BROS. have prepared a descriptive illustrated book of their various
Routes, which may be had gratis to passengers at any of their Booking Offices.

W. MATE & SONS, LTD., 58, Commercial Road, Bournemouth.   P.T.O.

Excursions leaflet issued during the period of horse-drawn vehicles

inn and the overall journey took about $1\frac{1}{2}$ hours. Mr H. H. Elliott has himself told us that his father laid down a strict schedule for the coaches of seven minutes per mile, including all stops and change-overs.

In 1888, however, the through railway line from Brockenhurst via Christchurch to Bournemouth was opened and the need for the Royal Blue service ceased. Besides the rail feeder service to and from Holmsley Station, Thomas Elliott was also a pioneer in the provision of local horse-bus services in Bournemouth, using wagonettes and pair or plain blue omnibuses and pair. From the late 1880s until about 1895 services were operated on the following three routes—

> The Square–Westbourne
> The Square–Boscombe
> Top of Richmond Hill–Winton Bank

On the last of these three routes, the horses were rested and fed at private stables in Talbot Road.

In the meanwhile, however, Mr Elliott had been developing his char-a-banc excursions from Bournemouth and a regular and varied programme was offered to places of scenic beauty and historic interest within the Bournemouth and New Forest area generally. These excursions were operated with 24-seat horse-drawn char-a-bancs and 18-seat coaches.

Summer was not the only time that Elliott's Royal Blue excursions were operated, as a contemporary account from the *Burnley Gazette* of 1 January 1908, describing Christmas in Bournemouth, reads as follows:

> Boarding one of Thomas Elliott's famous 'Royal Blue' stage coaches in which four spanking young steeds, displaying shining harnesses and buckles, stand restively in the Square, waiting for the crack of the whip, we start away for the New Forest. It is an ideal Christmas morning. The air is just sharp enough to make things look Christmassy. A bold red sun is glistening on the frosted windows, and the air rings with the musical clatter of the horses' hooves and the call of the post horn.
>
> Jack and Charlie, our coachmen, look well in their light slate hats, fawn coats, white gloves and brown leggings. Away we bound along the country roads until we reach the 'Cat & Fiddle', where a halt is called for refreshments. This old 'public' is over 600 years old, and nestles peacefully by the road side. To the call of the horn, we all mount again and away we speed for the Forest. Sitting alongside the 'coachie' on that

Royal Blue stage coach, we fancy ourselves living in the bygone years, when the L and NW, the GN and all other railways were unknown. When such a thing as a railway strike was an impossibility. When the only means of travel was by the old fashioned stage coach. Christmas Day in the New Forest; far from the madding crowd. All around us, as far as the eye can reach, are nothing but trees; oak, beech, ash and the poplar pine. Here and there we pass through a small village or other, centuries old. Sixty-five thousand acres, or rather more than 100 square miles, stretching away from North to South for 21 miles. The drive is a charming one, the old oak trees, the beautiful tints, the old villages together with charming companionship all tend to make this Christmas Day a memorable one. On our way we pass the residence of Miss Braddon, the popular authoress and Halwood, the country seat of the late Sir William Harcourt. Close upon one o'clock we reach Lyndhurst, the capital of the New Forest, 20 miles from Bournemouth. Here we halt for dinner at the 'Coach and Horses' where the genial landlord is waiting to greet us with his hearty 'Merry Christmas'. An hour later we are rattling away again along the road. Charlie, the coachie, cracking his jokes in his usual merry style. Soon the day begins to close, the sun shines, the long tall shadows cross our path, and another Christmas Day comes to an end. The silvery moon rises, coach lamps are lit, and we bound cheerfully along towards Bournemouth, all of one opinion that our Christmas Day in the New Forest was an experience we should never forget.

Charlie, the coachie mentioned in the above account, was Charles J. Pounds, who was employed as a four-in-hand driver with Royal Blue. He obtained his licence in 1893 and later became a char-a-banc driver; after the First World War in 1919 he formed his own motor coach business in Bournemouth—Charlies Cars.

The wheel went full circle when in 1966 Charlies Cars (Bournemouth) Ltd was bought by the Transport Holding Company and transferred to the Tilling Group of Companies, first having been bought by 'Shamrock & Rambler' in 1963 but operated as a separate entity. C. J. Pounds died in 1958. Jack, the other coachman mentioned in this press account was J. T. G. Elliott, later managing director of Elliott Bros.

At the height of the horse-drawn era about 200 horses were stabled at the Royal Blue Mews, with additional accommodation at Bourne Hall, Hotel Mews, Branksome Mews Stables near the Winter Gardens, and at the rear of the following Hotels: Belleview (which stood on the site of the Pavilion Bars), the Branksome, Prince of Wales, Pembroke, Tregonwell Arms, Victoria, and Westbourne. In addition, changes of horses were kept at Lyndhurst, Ringwood, New Milton and Fordingbridge.

In early October, at the end of the season, the annual sale of horses took place at Aldridges, St Martins Lane, London, and a special train of horse boxes conveyed the horses from Bournemouth Central Station to London, Waterloo Station. During the campaign for votes for women, a Royal Blue horse-drawn stage coach, driven by W. E. Elliott (Ted), conveyed supporters on a tour of Bournemouth.

The years 1902-3 saw the first motorised public service vehicles, but it was not until 1911 that Elliott's Royal Blue began to change from horse-drawn to motor vehicles, the first being taxicabs based at Avenue Road. One can sympathise with Thomas Elliott in resisting the change in view of his lifelong reliance on horses and one can imagine the restive impatience of the sons in seeking to utilise the new motor vehicles. It was in 1911 that the family business received a hard blow when on 28 January, Thomas Elliott died aged 53 years as a delayed result of a kick received from a horse, after an eventful and successful life. He had the reputation of being the foremost four-in-hand whip in the district and, besides being an expert driver, was considered to be a good employer.

A keen sportsman, Thomas Elliott was a member of the National Sporting Club and one of the founders and Secretary of the Bournemouth Cabman's Sick Benefit Club. He was a strong supporter of Bournemouth's annual parade of decorated horse-drawn coaches and an ardent competitor, winning first prize at local events in 1896, 1897, 1899, and 1900. He was survived by his wife, Mrs Elizabeth Elliott, his three sons and four daughters.

Perhaps the biggest tribute to him is the modern fleet of Royal Blue luxury coaches which daily provide a network of long distance express services by road throughout the South and West of England and stem directly from his enterprise in 1880.

It was, however, a family business and despite the tragedy of Thomas Elliott's early death, expansion continued, and in 1913 Royal Blue purchased their first two Dennis chars-a-banc with wooden wheels (licensed on 1 April 1913). These vehicles were painted dark (Royal) blue. The private hire car business was also considerably expanded at this time, and the speed of change-over can be imagined when it is realised that the last horse-drawn public carriage was disposed of in 1914.

THE FIRST WORLD WAR

The outbreak of war in 1915 did not bring about an immed-iate reduction in coaching, although all suitable horses were commandeered and sent to an Army re-mount depot.

In 1915 the business acquired twelve additional cars—two new 6-cylinder 25/30 hp Studebaker Cabriolets, three 16/24 hp Unic Cabriolets, four 16/24 hp Unic Landaulettes, and three 12/18 hp Unic Landaulettes—and these were added to the fleet of twelve already in use. These cars were advertised as being luxurious vehicles available for hire at taxi rates. All chauffeurs were in livery and it was suggested that the cars could be hired for town shopping, calling etc—at special rates.

A day and night taxi service was offered with charges as follows:

	s d		s d
Station—Central or		Dinner Parties, return	
West	1 6 (8p)	journey	4 0 (20p)
Theatre, return journey	5 0 (25p)	Hippodrome, return	
Church, return journey	4 0 (20p)	journey	6 0 (30p)
Winter Gardens, return		Balls, after midnight,	
journey	4 0 (20p)	return journey	7 6 (38p)

In addition, rates were offered for the daily hire of chauffeur-driven cars, of which the following are examples:

New Forest, Lyndhurst, Rufus Stone, Ringwood	£ 2 2s	od	(£2.10)
London (one day)	£ 7 10s	od	(£7.50)
Three days tour to Exeter and Torquay	£14 os	od	
Broadstone	16s	od	(80p)
Winchester	£ 3 10s	od	(£3.50)
Holmsley	£1 10s	od	(£1.50)

Royal Blue demanded a high standard from their staff, for every driver was required to be a trained mechanic, an expert driver, a man of exemplary character, and, above all, a total abstainer. It was claimed that 'no man who is not a total abstainer is driving a Royal Blue coach'. The staff wore a uniform in Royal Blue with gold facings; and the 22-seat coaches carried a conductor, a condition imposed by Bournemouth Town Council.

In 1915 Royal Blue owned fifteen char-a-bancs (of either 18- or 22-seat capacity) which the firm publicly described as motor coaches. They were painted in one of two liveries, light or sky blue. The vehicles themselves were claimed to be luxuriously upholstered, so that the longest trip could be taken without the slightest fatigue. Daimler 45 hp Silent Knight vehicles were the mainstay of the fleet, which also included some vehicles of 'Selden' manufacture.

Garages were located at 'The Royal Blue Garage', Avenue Lane, The Square; 'Royal Blue Garage', Wharf Road; and at 11 Talbot Road, Winton. Local agents were appointed to book passengers for the tours and Royal Blue were, in turn, agents for Thos Cook & Son and other principal travel agents. The departure point for all tours was The Square, and in 1916 the following selection was being offered:

Tour No	Destination	Fare		Dep Time
1.	Southampton, Winchester and Romsey	10s 6d	(53p)	Daily 10.30
2.	Salisbury and Stonehenge	10s 6d	(53p)	Daily 10.30
3.	Weymouth and Dorchester	7s	(35p)	Daily 10.30
4.	Day excursion around the New Forest	7s	(35p)	Daily 10.30
5.	Swanage and Corfe Castle	7s	(35p)	Daily 10.30
6.	Sherborne	8s 6d	(43p)	Mon Thurs 10.30
7.	Fordingbridge, Salisbury and Shaftesbury	10s 6d	(53p)	Tues Fri 10.30
8.	Round the New Forest, Lynd-hurst, Rufus Stone, Ring-wood	5s	(25p)	Daily 2.30
9.	Corfe Castle	5s	(25p)	Daily 2.30
10.	Milford-on-Sea, Lymington, Brockenhurst and Lynd-hurst	6s	(30p)	Daily 2.30
11.	Lulworth Cove	5s	(25p)	Daily 2.30
12.	Forest Village of Burley	4s	(20p)	Daily 2.30
13.	Blandford	5s	(25p)	Daily 2.30

War-time conscription took W. E. Elliott into the Royal Naval

Air Service in 1915, and during the same year H. H. Elliott joined the Royal Flying Corps, becoming an instructor at the Central Flying School. The former lost his life at the age of 28, when, as an Air Mechanic, First Engineer, he was the second crewman in a seaplane which failed to return to its base after a patrol on 14 May 1917. This was the second blow to the family and to the business in six years but it is a measure of their courage and resilience that they continued to expand despite these unhappy circumstances.

The third brother, J. T. G. Elliott, managed the business during the war and turned the Repair Works in Norwich Avenue (where all body and chassis repairs were carried out) into an armaments works which he supervised. Subsequently, he became a joint managing director of the business, from which he retired in 1934. He lived in Bournemouth until his death on 26 October 1963.

Restrictions on supplies led to Royal Blue using paraffin as a substitute fuel. The fleet was reduced by seven coaches, which were commandeered and purchased outright by the military authorities, and three Daimlers actually served in France. The drivers went with the commandeered vehicles and were enlisted in the Mechanical Transport section of the Royal Army Service Corps.

Undoubtedly the war acted as a spur to the development of the motor vehicle, and immediately after the cessation of hostilities in 1918 the business of reconstituting Royal Blue was put in hand. A garage was opened in Holdenhurst Road and was known as 'Elliott's Motor Vehicle Depot' (it is now the garage and offices of Shamrock and Rambler) and it was here that the majority of the Royal Blue coaches were garaged and running repairs carried out. The Lansdowne Garage was acquired by Elliott's and used for supplying taxis and private hire cars.

CHAPTER TWO

ELLIOTT BROS (BOURNEMOUTH) LTD 1919-1930

IN 1919 chance once again took a hand in the fortunes of the business in the form of a railway strike, which resulted in Royal Blue starting an experimental weekend service to London for return traffic from Bournemouth only. Originally planned to operate between Easter and Whitsun, circumstances and public demand led to the continuation of the service throughout the summer season. Additional vehicles were required and by the end of 1919 the fleet consisted of twenty-five motor coaches.

In 1919 Royal Blue also established their very popular Isle of Wight Tour. Passengers were taken by coach to Lymington, thence by boat to the Island, while the coaches were shipped across in barges. On the other side, coach and passengers recombined to make a complete circuit of the Isle of Wight, then returned to the mainland and Bournemouth in the same manner as they had come. But after a few years, Royal Blue built a garage in Mill Road, Yarmouth, so that one or two coaches could be stationed on the Isle of Wight, with the necessary drivers, and the tour was then carried out by Bournemouth-based vehicles as far as Lymington, boat to Yarmouth, and Island-based vehicles for the trip round the Isle of Wight.

The success of the London service in 1919 prompted the resumption in 1920 of a weekly Bournemouth–London service for the conveyance of passengers originating at either terminal. Arrangements were made for Thos Cook & Sons to act as booking agents, and, indeed, the London terminal was established near the Thos Cook & Sons office at 125 Pall Mall. As a result of the coal crisis, which affected rail services, and continuing public demand, the service was increased to twice weekly during the summer of 1920. During that year a former aircraft factory at Rutland Road, Bournemouth, was bought, suitably enlarged and equipped, and put into use as a repair works and garage, with accommodation for 60–100 coaches. A further important event was the change in livery from light to dark blue. In 1921

Fleet name display, 1922

the business and vehicles of Mark Briant's 'White Heather' undertaking were acquired; and their Daimler vehicles were rebuilt, fitted with coach bodies, and repainted in Royal Blue livery.

A LIMITED COMPANY

The business was rapidly expanding, and, anticipating further progress, it is not surprising that the family reorganised it, forming a private limited company to be known as Elliott Brothers (Bournemouth) Ltd on 10 May 1921. The life managing directors were H. H. and J. T. G. Elliott and, together with Mrs E. E. Elliott, they owned and controlled the new company, of which Mr H. W. Rollings was general manager and Mr A. E. Kinks the secretary.

Public demand required a further increase in the Bournemouth–London service, and when it restarted for the 1921 summer season it was on a daily basis with departures at 10.00 a.m. from each end; but even this was insufficient and additional timings were introduced at 2.00 p.m. in each direction. The fare for the through journey was 15s (75p) single or 25s (125p) return. Although passengers were being conveyed from London, Metropolitan licence plates were not obtained until 28 July 1921, by which time they had become compulsory. As a matter of interest, Royal Blue was the second provincial company to be granted Metropolitan plates in London for a long-distance service, the first being Chapmans of Eastbourne. This service was a pioneer coach service, the first operated over the route from Bournemouth, London, or any intermediate town.

It was a 'quality' service, passengers receiving individual attention and the unheard of luxury of a rug. Undoubtedly, the service caught the imagination of the public, who, denied any opportunity of seeing the beauties of their own country-side, except by train, showed their appreciation by booking every available seat for weeks ahead. Luggage was carried in luggage cars which followed the coaches.

At about this time, in order to keep drivers employed during the slack winter months, several 2 ton and 6 ton lorries were acquired and operated for goods haulage at competitive rates. But this venture did not prove successful and was allowed to die out.

In 1922, in conjunction with the Dunlop Rubber Co, pneumatic tyres were fitted on the coaches. In this year also the Company obtained licences from Bournemouth Corporation to operate local stage services, for which twelve Daimler 'Y' type chassis with Christopher Dodson bodies were ordered. But this move led to an agreement dated 1 February 1924 with Hants & Dorset Motor Services Ltd (who took over the purchase of the vehicles, paying Elliott Bros in cash and shares) that 'Hants & Dorset' would not operate tours from Bournemouth and Elliott Bros would not operate local stage services.

Other operators were quick to introduce long-distance coach

Page 35 J. T. G. Elliott with stage coach at Corfe Castle

Page 36 (above) teams at Ringwood with char-a-bancs, 1907, the brothers
(J. T. G., W. T., and H. H.) Elliott driving

(left) Royal Blue stage coach
in the 1890s, driven by the
late C. J. Pounds

(right) one of the two
original Dennis char-a-bancs.
Note the wooden wheels

services and despite considerable research, all that can safely be said now is that Elliott Bros were among the first to start regular services, as opposed to the purely 'party' type of operations.

It is suggested that a true express service is, in fact, a motorised reincarnation of the original horse-drawn mail coach, regularly operated to a published timetable, with stage to stage fares, and individual bookings, single and return. As to the definition of 'long distance', the service should run between towns or cities and preferably have one or more intermediate towns on the way.

The first long-distance services, such as that operated by Elliott Bros between Bournemouth and London, provided for the conveyance of passengers between terminals only. It is generally accepted that Greyhound Motors Limited of Bristol (now part of the Bristol Omnibus Company Limited) began the first regular express service, as defined above, on 11 February 1925 between Bristol and London. This service carried both passengers booked between terminals and passengers from stage to stage on the journey. It was in fact a rebirth of the old stage and mail coaches in everything except the vehicles used. These were very advanced for the time with 'giant pneumatic' tyres on the front wheels and coach-built bodies resplendent with 'Lincrusta' ceilings, French polished panelling, and mock curtains. This service, which received considerable publicity in the national press, was another element in 'triggering off' a quite fantastic period of unregulated development and competition only brought to an end by the Road Traffic Act of 1930.

'PIRATES'

In order to appreciate the competition at this time, one must remember that after the First World War many young men with driving experience had come out of the armed forces. Many had saved their service gratuities and with the help of hire-purchase companies were trying their hand at running ordinary

C

omnibus services. In London the services were dubbed 'Pirate buses' and were operated in competition with the routes of the London General Omnibus Co Ltd and the tramway undertakings. Although there were one or two exceptions, the 'pirates', as one might expect from the name, ran without control as to route and times, deliberately exploiting any deficiency in the regular 'frequency' services provided by the established operators.

These were colourful times and competition was allowed absolutely free range. A 'pirate' bus would start out in the morning with a box of destination boards and route numbers, commencing operation by watching a particular London General service in order to find a gap in the regular headway. As soon as this occurred, up would go the board for that destination, with the London General route number displayed without the slightest suggestion of 'by your leave'. Away the pirate would go, picking up passengers at every bus stop. Naturally, the London General driver behind would sense the absence of passengers, or be told of the pirate by the inspector; he would speed up, overtake the pirate, and recapture the 'road'. Pirate bus drivers adopted every kind of trick to obtain traffic and were known, when beset by several 'General' buses and with only a few passengers on board, to conveniently turn off the petrol and feign a breakdown. As soon as the last passenger had had his money refunded and left the bus, the pirate would again hide down a side-turning and repeat his tactics.

The 1924 London Traffic Act brought these days to a close by introducing a system of licences, and the 'pirates' one by one sold out to the London General Omnibus Company. Very naturally, a number of pirate operators, having acquired practical experience in this way, decided to invest their gains in longer-distance bus or coach operations. By 1928 the chassis manufacturers and body builders had begun to produce a type of vehicle which enabled long-distance services to be both comfortable and reliable and this combination of factors resulted in services being introduced on a wide scale in the years 1925-30.

No licensing system existed outside London, except for the local hackney carriage regulations, and, in practice, one simply bought a coach and started to operate, with or without local authority approval. Many and varied were the names of the operators and, as previously in London, competition was intense and unregulated. Fares were cut to the bone, operators vying with each other to offer the lowest rate.

An example of the price-cutting war was the service between London and Plymouth via Salisbury—420 miles return journey. This route, which also served Torquay, was begun by Royal Blue on 26 May 1928 and operated once daily throughout the year with minor adjustments to times until 1930 when a second timing (not passing through Salisbury) was introduced on 18 July.

Fares were set at 20s (100p) single and 35s (175p) return and were maintained at this level until November 1930. In October 1930, the Royal Arsenal Co-operative Society Ltd reduced the fare between Torquay and London to 12s 6d (63p) single and 17s 6d (88p) return. Royal Blue endeavoured to get all operators to maintain prices but one by one they fell into line with the 'cut fare' and on 13 November Royal Blue announced that as and from 1 December they would charge 10s (50p) single and 15s (75p) return. This resulted in a meeting of operators who agreed on standard fares of 17s 6d (88p) single and 27s 6d (138p) return for that winter and, at a subsequent meeting, 20s (100p) single and 35s (175p) return. These prices were maintained until 19 May 1931, when RACS Ltd announced summer fares of 17s 6d (88p) single and 30s (150p) return, although until this date they had maintained the agreed fares. The other operators preserved the agreed fares and in the final event RACS Ltd did not obtain a road service licence for this route, under the provisions of the Road Traffic Act of 1930.

Naturally, competition in fares and the bitterness it engendered communicated itself to the drivers; racing and cutting-in became rife. There were one or two serious accidents and generally the position deteriorated as a result of the mushroom growth of operators and the lack of organisation, particularly in vehicle maintenance. There was no standard of service. Overworking of drivers was carried to quite scandalous lengths, men being despatched on, say, a Friday night to cover journeys the next morning from a terminus hundreds of miles away.

To find specific examples of the battles which were fought on the roads is difficult, but the results were often quite disastrous. One specific incident involved a Gilford 6-wheeler of 'Superways', which took the hump-back bridge at Fenny Bridges, Devon, at 50–60 mph, left the road and plunged into a wood. A number of passengers were injured and some killed and to this day there are marks where the hedgerow and trees were ploughed down.

The Local Authority licensing system was the only measure of control prior to the Road Traffic Act of 1930, and was exercised by those local authority areas where the Hackney Carriage Regulations were in force. Any operators desirous of providing public transport had to obtain a licence plate from the appropriate local authority and affix it to their vehicles. Such a licence could be granted or refused as the council saw fit, and to it could be attached whatever conditions relating to equipment of vehicles and any other matters that the council deemed appropriate.

Although the intentions were good, the system became an absurdity, as each authority acted in isolation and sometimes in contradiction to neighbours on either side. A case in point was the matter of 'life-guards'—gate-like structures attached to a vehicle chassis below the high body sides to fill the gap between the front and rear wheels. In theory this was to prevent people falling under the vehicle, but it was of doubtful value in practice. One can imagine the plight of a Royal Blue vehicle travelling on a route which passed from an area requiring the fitting of life-guards to one which had decided against them! Furthermore, the mounting of the 'approval plates' of all the authorities on every vehicle in the fleet became an impossible task. The backs of the vehicles were literally covered with plates of all sizes and shapes.

By 1926, Royal Blue were operating thirty-four 'Y' type 26-seater Daimlers, twenty CK type Daimlers with 14–26 seats, and a further eighteen 26-seater coaches on AEC chassis. Most of the bodies were built by London Lorries Ltd of Kentish Town, London, NW5, the original designers and manufacturers of the patent, quadruple-purpose, all-weather, saloon coach body. In addition, eight Rolls-Royce, twenty-two 6-cylinder Daimler, and eight 6-cylinder Wolseley cars were retained for private hire and a Rolls-Royce chassis was used as an emergency breakdown tender, carrying full equipment, tools, and appliances. All coaches, except those needed for winter services, were stored at Rutland Road, Bournemouth, at the end of the season, and it was during the winter that most of the overhaul and reconditioning work took place. The company's main stores were also located at this garage. During the 1920s a newspaper parcels delivery service was operated for several years between Southampton Station, Bournemouth, and Weymouth, utilising Rolls-Royce tenders.

Garages were located at 68 Holdenhurst Road, Lansdowne Garage, 33 Old Christchurch Road, and Post Office Road. Other garages were principally used for housing the private cars. The premises at Avenue Lane near The Square were used for the cars engaged on private hire work.

Licensing and police inspection were carried out at Poole and Bournemouth and coaches operating into the Metropolitan area (London) were subject to Scotland Yard tests. The company's main booking office, costing and records department, and registered office were at 68 Holdenhurst Road, Bourne-mouth. A wide network of booking agents was set up, and in Bournemouth a series of tobacco and confectionery shops was established by the company to act as coach booking offices, displaying Royal Blue posters and publicity, in addition to their ordinary retail trade. They were located at Richmond Hill (now National Provincial Bank), Commercial Road (now H. Samuel's, Jewellers), and 33 Old Christchurch Road (now Boots the Chemists). Many of Bournemouth's leading hotels also acted as agents.

Six- and eight-day inclusive tours, arranged by Thos Cook & Sons, were operated to a variety of places in the West Country, utilising Royal Blue long-distance services from London in conjunction with the Company's daily local excursions. Elliott Bros were pioneers in this field of touring.

All drivers had to pass a very rigid company test, and all conductors had to be qualified drivers. During 1926, the company's coaches covered some 1,250,000 miles with practically no mechanical defects.

DEVELOPMENT OF EXPRESS SERVICES

On the threshold of the development of express road services, the company was in a unique position in the centre of the south coast of England and able to branch out in many directions, east, west, or north. Small wonder that in 1928, when the company realised the demand existing for long-distance road services, that they set about making applications to run to a large number of important cities and towns such as London, Plymouth, Birmingham, and Bristol. Licences were successfully sought to provide services from both London and Bournemouth to many of these terminals, and, to complete the framework, Royal Blue then applied to all the intermediate town councils and licensing authorities for permission to pick up and set down at points on the way.

In the same year the vehicle manufacturers produced the type of chassis suitable for such services; the vehicles had twin rear wheels of smaller diameter, thus enabling a lower chassis to be built. About this time, to distinguish the long-distance services from local tours, Elliott Bros adopted the trading name of 'Royal Blue Automobile Services' for their express coach business.

As an example of the licensing procedure, the London–Bournemouth service was improved by obtaining local authority 'plates' in Winchester (Jan 1928), Basingstoke (Mar 1928), Camberley (May 1928), Christchurch (Jan 1929), Eastleigh (Feb 1929), Bagshot (Mar 1929), and Southampton (May 1929) after an appeal. The service was now truly an express one in

the present sense of the term, but obvious success soon has its
imitators and between 1928 and the enactment of the Road
Traffic Act in 1930, competition appeared on the London–
Bournemouth route from Highways, Cambrian, Tourist,
Timpsons, George Ewer & Co, RACS, Main Lines, Shamrock &
Rambler, and Keith & Boyle. These operators obtained some
but not all of the local authority plates, but were never successful
in giving the route the coverage provided by Elliott Bros. The
only ones still remaining on the London–Bournemouth route
are Timpsons and George Ewer & Co.

Other operators between Southampton and London in
addition to the London–Bournemouth operators who had
operating rights in Southampton were Valley Queen Services
and Modern Travel Ltd, who soon gave up the struggle, leaving
'Tourist' as the sole Southampton-based operator of express
services. Tourist Coaches were an important constituent in the
present network and the history of this company is described in
Chapter 4.

Following their policy of expansion, Elliott Bros. introduced
the following services during this critical period:

    1928 London–Salisbury–Plymouth. Saturdays
    1928 Bournemouth–Dorchester–Plymouth
    1928 Bournemouth–Yeovil–Ilfracombe
    1928 London–Bristol–Weston-super-Mare
    1929 Bournemouth–Coventry–Birmingham
    1929 Bournemouth–Portsmouth–Margate
    1929 Bournemouth–Bristol

(The London–Bournemouth route was already in operation, prior to
1928.)

This rapid development in 1928-9 was sparked-off by two
quite separate factors. One, the foundation in April 1925 of
London Coastal Coaches and, two, the increasing realisation by
the more far-sighted operators that the Royal Commission on
Transport, which was then sitting, was bound to recommend
the passing of some legislation to restrict free competition. It
was, therefore, essential to stake claims on any routes where
operation was thought to be worthwhile.

In April 1929, Elliott Bros started the Bournemouth–Margate

service, and it is an interesting commentary on the keenly competitive conditions of those days that Southdown Motor Services Ltd started their Dover–Bournemouth service on 1 June 1929, ie within three months of Elliott Bros' operations through their territory. Further introductions were Southsea–Oxford–Birmingham, 1 March 1930; Plymouth–Birmingham, 1 April 1930; and Ilfracombe–Birmingham, Portsmouth–Romsey–Salisbury (linking into London service), and a London–Bournemouth late night service, all introduced on 16 June 1930.

On the tours side of the business, Elliott Bros had maintained and improved their local tour network to scenic and historic points within 100 miles of Bournemouth. The provision of coaches for private hire was still an important part of the business.

In The Square—the heart of the town—Elliott Bros shared with the Hants & Dorset Motor Services Ltd one of the latest and most up to date bus stations of the period. It was erected at a cost of £1,000,000 in 1929 and replaced the terminal previously situated at 68-70 Holdenhurst Road.

For the operation of the long-distance services, the company had agents or resident inspectors in all leading towns. In London the booking agents were London Coastal Coaches Ltd and their sub-agents, who, in the case of Bournemouth, booked exclusively for the services provided by Elliott Bros.

LONDON COASTAL COACHES

The formation of London Coastal Coaches Ltd in 1925 was an important event, in which Royal Blue participated. The beginnings of this enterprise go back to the very early 1920s, when as 'London & Coastal Motor Services', a small group of pioneers, which included Pickfords, Southdown, and Thomas Tilling, began running vehicles to and from the South and East coasts, using Pickfords office in High Holborn as the starting point. The present company was formed in April 1925 by five large 'Associated Companies', viz East Kent Road Car Co Ltd,

Maidstone & District Motor Services Ltd, The National Omnibus & Transport Co Ltd, Southdown Motor Services Ltd, and United Automobile Services Ltd, and certain other smaller companies, one of which was Royal Blue.

London Coastal Coaches' terminus was at Lupus Street, not far from Vauxhall Bridge. An open yard formed the station from which all departures took place, a private house at the entrance to the yard being used as the main office. The present Victoria Coach Station in Buckingham Palace Road, owned by London Coastal Coaches, dates from 1932 and is today the centre from which practically all the express services run by the Associated Companies depart to nearly every point in Great Britain. On the busier days, as many as 1,500 coaches depart in twenty-four hours.

Two other principal operators who were agents for Royal Blue were Southern National in Ilfracombe, and Western National in Plymouth. Southdown, East Kent, and Maidstone & District booked solely for Elliott Bros along the coast from Portsmouth to Margate.

Supervision of services on the way was carried out by a staff of travelling inspectors, who were almost entirely former police officers.

In January 1930, Mr C. H. Preece joined the management side of Elliott Bros, having formerly been with Holland Motor Coaches of Southampton, the Royal Blue controlling agents for Southampton and district. He was one of the original London 'Pirate Bus' operators. Mr Preece was to play a major part in the development and consolidation of Royal Blue services from 1930 to 1965, so much so that they have been referred to as 'Preece's Coachways'. When the Western/Southern National Companies acquired Royal Blue in 1935 he continued with the new owners, ultimately becoming Traffic Manager (Commercial) of the combined undertaking. His main contributions were the planning of services, their negotiation with the railways and other interests, and the obtaining of the necessary licences before the traffic commissioners.

It can be said fairly, that the network of Express coach services throughout Great Britain was largely a copy of the pattern formulated by Royal Blue.

The Road Traffic Act became law on 1 August 1930 and amongst other things it provided for the setting up of traffic areas and traffic commissioners; also a system of licensing for services, vehicles, drivers, and conductors. The strife between operators on the roads was now transferred to the commissioners courts and the road service licence became a coveted and vital document. The first additions to the Elliott Bros' network after the passing of the Act were extensions to Derby and Nottingham introduced on 1 September 1930, but not in accordance with the new procedure.

At the passing of the Act, Elliott Bros were operating eleven express routes, mainly radiating from Bournemouth, some, of course, with a number of timings each day :

London–Salisbury–Plymouth
Bournemouth–Dorchester–Plymouth
Bournemouth–Yeovil–Ilfracombe
London–Bristol–Weston-super-Mare
London–Bournemouth
Bournemouth–Coventry–Birmingham
Bournemouth–Portsmouth–Margate
Bournemouth–Bristol
Southsea–Oxford–Birmingham
Plymouth–Birmingham
Ilfracombe–Birmingham

The financial crisis and slump of 1929-30 left Royal Blue unscathed, and, in fact, 1930 was a particularly good year. Generally, public transport tends to thrive during hard times, when private cars or holidays abroad are too expensive.

CHAPTER THREE

THE ROAD TRAFFIC ACT OF 1930 AND ITS REPERCUSSIONS 1930-1935

CASES IN THE TRAFFIC COURTS

THE years 1930–1935 were eventful and interesting in the history of all transport undertakings and of Royal Blue in particular. In effect, the Road Traffic Act imposed new terms of reference on all providers of public transport. Generally speaking, the industry welcomed the 1930 Act and, as far as bus and coach operation is concerned, it is noteworthy that the main provisions, slightly modified in some instances, are still applicable. But the details, the setting of precedents, the nice interpretation of clauses, all had to be fought out during the four or five years after the Act came into force. It was the era of the great legal battles, in which all the old ingenuity and strife of the 'pirate bus' days were transferred from the streets into the courts. Though perhaps more civilised, the struggle between operators was if anything sharper than in the pre-1930 days : if one's bus was passed on the road by another operator there was always another day to even the score, but if one's case in the traffic courts was lost to sharper wits and keener presentation the opportunity was gone for ever. It is not surprising that Royal Blue, with its ramifications all over the south and south-west and even up into the Midlands, became embroiled in major legal tussles, some of which were classics in the interpretation of the 1930 Act and set precedents which have been observed ever since. It is the main purpose of this chapter to sketch some of these great cases, which were never lacking in excitement and seldom in a sparkle of humour, since the leading legal figures of the day were briefed. Royal Blue employed Walter Monckton, KC for their early cases, and he later became Sir Walter and subsequently Lord Monckton, a member of the Government during and after the Second World War. With him as his 'junior' was Norman Fox Andrews, KC.

The 'Summation of Fares' case is perhaps the most important and the one for which Royal Blue will go down in legal history. In 1931, in an attempt to preserve their position, which had become very complicated following the passing of the 1930 Act, Elliott Bros (Bournemouth) Ltd applied in the West Midland Traffic Area for the following fifteen licences to cover what were, in effect, three trunk routes in the West Midlands Area:

Plymouth	–Derby	Southsea	–Derby
„	–Nottingham	„	–Nottingham
Paignton	–Derby	„	–Derby (2)
„	–Nottingham	„	–Birmingham
Ilfracombe	–Derby	Bournemouth	–Derby
„	–Nottingham	„	–Birmingham
Bournemouth	–Derby	„	–Nottingham
„	–Nottingham		

Each service had its own through faretable, all of which had to be attached to all applications to give the maximum combination of through-booking facilities—it was rather like a football-pool permutation on which the backer could not lose. Perhaps understandably, the traffic commissioners refused to accept these applications at a hearing on 31 July 1931 and asked for simplified applications to be submitted, confined to straightforward routes. Royal Blue accordingly re-submitted applications for three routes only, but took the sensible precaution of attaching to the applications such through fares on linking services as they had hitherto charged. The West Midland commissioners granted licences for these three trunk routes on 19 May 1932, but struck out all through fares when they found that Royal Blue proposed to interchange passengers at linking points; they enunciated the principle that licences should be restricted to the fares and operations strictly within the geographical confines of the route applied for only.

Royal Blue timetable cover for the London–Bournemouth service, 1932

The refusal of the 'through fares on connecting services' principle would have deprived Royal Blue of a substantial part of their existing traffic and left the way wide open for applications from competing operators; alternatively it would have necessitated Royal Blue applying for and operating through vehicles wherever they required through fares, with needless and uneconomic duplication of facilities. Elliott Bros accordingly lodged an appeal with the minister, whose subsequent decision was wholly favourable to them and established the following important principles :

(a)   Summation of fares on connecting services was permissible : if this was a straight summation of the fares of the two linked sections, no action was necessary on the licences but if the through fares were proposed at less than summation, then they could and should be attached to both of the licences affected.
(b)   The issue of through tickets was permissible.
(c)   The linking of services by through vehicle operation was also permissible.

The significance of this decision was demonstrated nearly thirty years later in 1960, when Associated Motorways encountered a similar difficulty, again with the West Midland traffic commissioners. Mr Preece, who had fought the original case as traffic manager for Elliott Bros in 1932, was able to enter the lists once again in 1960 and give evidence of the minister's decision in support of Associated Motorways, who won their point.

Elliott Bros' relations with the chairman of the West Midland traffic commissioners do indeed appear to have been strained and in appearing before him again on 20 May 1932, in a comparatively straightforward objection to the Birmingham & Midland Motor Omnibus Co Ltd, there occurred one of the most dramatic moments in the history of the traffic courts.

The Chairman, having heard only part of the BMMO case, and in the middle of Mr Fox Andrews' cross-examination of their witness, stopped the proceedings and granted the application. The transcript reads as follows :

CHAIRMAN : I don't think we want to take this any further. We feel the service is required from the Black Country to connect with the West of England and the application is granted.

MR FOX ANDREWS (for Elliott Bros): In spite of the fact that I desire to put a lot of other questions in cross-examination?

CHAIRMAN: We are satisfied that there is a need for this service.

MR FOX ANDREWS: In spite of my desire to continue, you stop my cross-examination, and grant the application?

CHAIRMAN: Yes.

MR FOX ANDREWS: I do want to get this absolutely clear upon the short-hand note that despite my desire to call evidence the application is granted.

CHAIRMAN: We have heard sufficient to feel that we are entitled to grant the application. There is a need for direct facilities and these are being granted to the existing operator in the West of England.

MR FOX ANDREWS: I want to make my submission crystal clear. It is being granted in spite of my opposition.

CHAIRMAN: We have never recognised Messrs Elliotts of Bournemouth as providing facilities from the Midlands to Weston and Paignton . . . I hope it is quite clear.

MR FOX ANDREWS: I am submitting (a) that I have a right to be here (b) that I have been prevented from taking the case.

CHAIRMAN: We are convinced that the service is necessary to the public.

END OF SITTING

Royal Blue of course made an appeal to the minister and, not surprisingly, won; even the Birmingham & Midland Motor Omnibus Co Ltd freely admitting that they had no special merit to justify preferential treatment at the expense of Elliott Bros. Both companies obtained the licences they had applied for and shortly afterwards there was a change in the chairmanship of the West Midland traffic commissioners.

Another important case in which Royal Blue were the main protagonists was that dealing with pre-booked private parties—the so-called 'Battle of Salisbury', in April 1933. For some time traffic commissioners had been somewhat exercised as to the interpretation of the 1930 Act in relation to private hire parties, other than those which clearly fell into the category of contract carriage operation. It is obvious that in most privately organised coach outings the sponsor collects separate contributions from those taking part and the traffic commissioners for the Southern Area were attempting to enforce a ruling that separate licences should therefore be applied for and obtained in respect of each private hire trip. The difficulties are apparent: to carry out such a procedure would mean that every private coach trip would have to be applied for several months in advance with full details of route and fares, so that publication in the traffic commissioners 'Notices & Proceedings' could take place, and the statutory period of three weeks for possible objections allowed for! Since many private parties are not organised until only a week or two before the event, and details such as route and fares are not finalised until the last few days by the hirer, it was obvious that so ponderous a procedure as that proposed by the traffic commissioners could not work in practice.

Elliott Bros agreed to act as 'guinea-pigs' in a test case, submitting appropriate applications to which Southdown Motor Services and a number of other operators lodged (agreed) objections. The matter was dealt with at a long involved hearing at Salisbury. The pomp and dignity of traffic court proceedings in these early days is nicely illustrated by the words of the late Mr Justice Wrottesley, then appearing as counsel for one of the objectors, who, in reference to a trip to the Derby stated, 'The applicant seeks to run to Epsom, where, I am instructed, horse-racing takes place'. Days of argument were spent in dealing with this case and its appeal, the final outcome being a ruling that licences are only required where separate fares are publicly advertised (ie in a shop-window, press advertisements, pamphlet, or parish magazine) by the organiser or operator of a pre-booked private party. It is a fine distinction which still gives rise to occasional difficulties with Women's Institute outings, skittle-match trips, rave, jive, or beat-group gatherings. Briefly, if you invite the general public to take part in a coach trip at separate fares or contributions, you must obtain a road service licence or you are breaking the law.

The last of the major issues involving Royal Blue was the 'Fan-Tail Tours' case, the original hearing of which took place in January 1934. The reader will probably require a few words in explanation of this strange term. With the development and growth of coach touring holidays, operators from the industrial and residential areas started applying for extended tours on trunk routes to various resorts, and including in their applications local tours for their clients while staying at the resorts—the 'fan-tail'. 'This peculiar animal, which has both feathers and a trunk',

Page 53 The Square, Bournemouth: (*above*) c 1904, with Royal Blue vehicles drawn up on 'the stand' and trams in the background; (*below*) eighteen years later there were still trams and Royal Blue coaches

Page 54 (*above*) motor coach with body by London Lorries Limited, 1921-2.
Note the fleet name display; (*below*) Rolls-Royce parcels 'pick-up'

to quote the words of learned counsel at one of the hearings. The threat of the fan-tail tour to existing operators was twofold: first, the abstraction of traffic from established express services between the point of origin and the holiday resort; second, the denial to the local tours operator of traffic which he might legitimately expect from an influx of holidaymakers and would certainly receive if the passengers travelled by express coach or by rail.

By one of these quirks which so often attend upon human affairs, the test case arose from an application by Feather Bros of Bradford for a fan-tail tour from Bradford to Torquay, with local tours ex-Torquay. The opportunity of objecting was almost missed; the railways, who usually scrutinised 'Notices & Proceedings' with eagle eyes and were quick to object to anything which threatened their long-distance traffic, unaccountably overlooked this application, and the objection therefore rested with the traffic manager of Royal Blue, who chanced to see it in a North-western Area publication of the traffic commissioners. It was agreed that Royal Blue would pursue the case on behalf of Associated Motorways. During the proceedings, there occurred one of those 'passages-at-arms' which so often brighten English legal procedure, when Mr Preece who was taking the case referred to opposing counsel as 'my friend'. Counsel, who had recently figured in a prominent murder trial, took umbrage at this familiarity, saying this term was used in courts of law between lawyers only. On being asked how he would like to be addressed, the chairman, Sir William Chamberlain, intervened with, 'I suggest you call him Comrade!' This fan-tail case was one of a series and finally, on appeal, the minister ruled that the local tours in such operations should be restricted to one only, any additional tours to be carried out by the local operator either directly with his own vehicles or using the vehicle of the fan-tail operator 'on hire'. This restriction still applies. The 'trunk' portion of such applications is, of course, subject to normal traffic court procedure—proof of need by the applicant, objection by the existing express operator if he feels his facilities are being damaged.

D

Behind all these major cases there were the run-of-the-mill applications by Royal Blue to obtain licences under the 1930 Act for the services they were already operating; the initial application for Elliott Bros' services took a total of some eight days to hear. The company had to apply for, fight, and appeal against 'claim-jumping' all along the line to gain their licences. All in all, they were four very busy years for Elliott Bros and very costly ones too; during one year no less than £7,000 was spent in legal expenses. Nevertheless, the cost was considered to have been more than justified, as the grant of the licences firmly established the company as the major operator of long-distance services in the South-west and in many cases the sole operator on particular routes. The proceedings before the traffic commissioners had worked to the company's advantage by securing the withdrawal of some competitors' services, and establishing working agreements with others.

CO-ORDINATION AND OTHER EVENTS

But other important developments were taking place in these crucial years, apart from legal issues. In January 1931, an attempt was made by the Devon General Omnibus & Touring Co Ltd to tap Royal Blue's west-country traffic, by establishing a limited stop service from Torquay to Bournemouth, twice daily, connecting at the latter point with Greyhound Motors Ltd to Southampton and London. Objection was lodged by Elliott Bros and the traffic commissioners refused licences for 'Devon General' and 'Greyhound', whose facilities ceased in June 1931.

Also in 1931 were established the Central and Regional Fares Committees, largely at the instigation of that pioneer of the omnibus industry, Mr S. E. Garcke. These Committees co-ordinated and regulated the level of fares on all express services and day tours out of London, day tour fares being fixed at the same level as express day return fares (except for race meetings, where a free hand was given to tour fares). Apart from the Second World War period, these fares committees have functioned continuously since 1931, except that the Central Fares

Committee was disbanded in 1956 as it appeared to have out-lived its usefulness.

Since 1930, Royal Blue had been engaged in a lengthy dispute with Southdown Motor Services and the East Kent Road Car Co regarding services along the South Coast. Both companies had opposed the Royal Blue application for a licence. On 11 March 1932 two events occurred, one sad and the other favourable in the fortunes of the company. Mrs Elizabeth Elliott, 75 years old, who had taken an active interest in the business until her final illness, died on the same day that Royal Blue, under the guidance of the traffic commissioners for the South-eastern Area, reached a co-ordination agreement with Southdown and East Kent, establishing the South Coast Express Service.

The agreement, under which each operator took approx-imately one-third of the route in respect of both mileage and receipts, is still observed in the form concluded in 1932. In effect, Portsmouth was established as the eastern boundary point for Royal Blue, though vehicles of all three companies continue to work throughout the length of the route from Bournemouth to Margate.

August of 1932 saw a co-ordinated timetable with Greyhound Motor Services Ltd on the London–Bristol–Weston-super-Mare route. Greyhound had started a Bristol–London service on 11 February 1925, and also operated for a short while between London and Bournemouth (from November 1930 to June 1931) until the refusal of their licence as indicated above. In October 1933 the joint Royal Blue/Greyhound operation was extended to a pooling of mileage and receipts and Royal Blue retained their interest on this basis until October 1965, when the complete route was taken over by the Bristol Omnibus Co. The latter, as the Bristol Tramways & Carriage Co Ltd, had acquired a controlling interest in Greyhound Motor Services in 1929, prior to complete acquisition in 1936.

A further co-ordination agreement was negotiated in 1933 with South Midland Motor Services relating to the Portsmouth/Bournemouth–Birmingham route. So, behind the façade of the spectacular legal battles, the true spirit and intentions of the 1930 Act were being quietly carried out.

The Royal Blue timetable leaflets at this time included the following note:

WHAT ROYAL BLUE SERVICE STANDS FOR

An organisation which has ever before it an ambition to serve the Public—this service taken at its fullest and real meaning, has a task to accomplish of no mean order; such is our constant aim, however, towards which every member of our staff is always taught to look; it is a task which is never complete, for our ideal always marches ahead of our achievement.

We have but three axioms, your safety, your comfort and your convenience; to obtain them we spare no effort. Our coaches are the finest we can obtain! They and their drivers are licensed by The Traffic Commissioners through whose areas they pass, and may therefore be taken to be absolutely safe. The work of cleaning and maintaining the coaches never ceases night or day.

The result we leave to your judgment as an experienced traveller.

British all through—and proud of it.

The sober dignity of this advertisement contrasts with modern high-powered slick-catch-phrase advertising, liberally sprinkled with lavish offers of free gifts. But then it must be recalled Great Britain at this time was still mistress of the world's greatest Empire and a sober statement of intent, coupled with a little jingoism, were quite sufficient.

In April 1932, the 30 mph maximum speed limit was imposed on all public service vehicles, a rather unfortunate restriction, since the Road Traffic Act of 1930 had in itself eliminated the dangerous racing and excessive speeds associated with the unrestricted competition of the 1920s. This 30 mph limit was to restrict the speed at which express coach services could be scheduled for the next 29 years.

The year 1933 was a very full and eventful one for Elliott Bros. During its course consideration was given to floating the undertaking as a public company, but rejected. But further expansion came about with the purchase of Traveller Saloon Coaches of Plymouth, who operated between Plymouth and Portsmouth, and who the previous year had themselves purchased Olympic Services Ltd of Portsmouth, operating between Portsmouth and Bristol. This eliminated the only competition

OLYMPIC
Motor Services Ltd.,
8, KENT ROAD, SOUTHSEA.

SALOON COACH SERVICE
BETWEEN

BRISTOL, BATH, SOUTHAMPTON,
Portsmouth AND Southsea.

TWICE DAILY (SUNDAYS INCLUDED.)

From Bristol Read times down		STAGES.	From Southsea Read times up	
a.m.	p.m.		p.m.	p.m.
8.30	2.30	BRISTOL (Prince St. Road Travel Bureau)	1.45	7.45
9.10	3.10	BATH (Cleveland Bridge)	1.5	7.5
9.40	—	BRADFORD-ON-AVON (Baths)	—	6.35
9.50	—	TROWBRIDGE (Town Hall)	—	6.25
10.5	—	WESTBURY (Market Place)	—	6.10
—	3.55	FROME (Market Place)	12.20	—
10.20	4.20	WARMINSTER (Market Place)	11.55	5.55
11.25	5.25	SALISBURY (Market Place)	10.50	4.50
12.35	6.35	SOUTHAMPTON (Pound Tree Rd. or Cumberland Pl.)	9.40	3.40
1.35	7.35	PORTSMOUTH (Angerstein Road)	8.40	2.40
1.40	7.40	„ (St. Michael's Church)	8.35	2.35
1.45	7.45	SOUTHSEA (Clarence Pier)	8.30	2.30
p.m.	p.m.		a.m.	p.m.
Arrive.			Depart.	

WINTER FARES.

Light Figures—Single Fares. Heavy Figures—Return Fares.	Bristol.	Bath.	Bradford.	Trowbridge.	Westbury.	Frome.	Warminster.	Salisbury.	Southampton.	Portsmouth or Southsea.
	s. d.	s. d.	s. d.	s. d.	s. d.	s. d.	s. d.	s. d.	s. d.	s. d.
BRISTOL ...	—	1 0	2 3	2 6	3 0	2 6	3 6	5 0	7 0	8 6
BATH ...	2 0	—	1 3	1 8	2 0	2 0	2 6	4 0	6 0	7 6
BRADFORD ...	3 8	2 3	—	1 0	1 0	—	1 3	3 3	5 3	7 0
TROWBRIDGE ...	4 2	2 10	2 0	—	1 0	—	1 0	3 0	4 9	6 9
WESTBURY ...	5 0	3 4	2 0	2 0	—	—	1 0	2 6	4 9	6 6
FROME ...	4 2	3 4	—	—	—	—	2 0	2 0	4 9	6 9
WARMINSTER ...	5 10	4 2	2 1	2 1	2 0	2 0	—	2 3	4 0	6 0
SALISBURY ...	8 4	6 8	5 5	5 0	4 2	4 2	3 8	—	2 6	4 0
SOUTHAMPTON ...	11 0	10 0	8 6	7 6	7 0	7 6	6 6	4 6	—	2 1
PORTSMOUTH or SOUTHSEA ...	14 0	12 6	11 6	10 10	10 6	10 10	9 8	6 0	3 4	—

GENERAL INFORMATION.

ADVANCE BOOKINGS.—Bookings may be made in advance, either for Single or Return Journeys.

RETURN TICKETS.—These are available for 3 months only from date of issue. Undated Return Tickets should be notified to the Operators on the appropriate card supplied, giving at least 3 clear days' notice of return. Unless this notice is given seats cannot be guaranteed. Where possible passengers are advised to book their date of return when taking ticket.

FARES.—Adult Fares are as shown in the Schedule of Fares. Children under 5 years of age free. Between the ages of 5 and 14 travel at half fare.

DOGS.—Small Dogs only will be carried when clean and not a nuisance to passengers.

LUGGAGE.—One suit-case or similar package will be allowed free to each passenger.

BOOKING AGENTS.—Passengers are advised to book their seats in advance through an authorised Booking Agency to ensure accommodation.

DAILY CONNECTIONS from BRISTOL TO LONDON, COVENTRY, BIRMINGHAM, WESTON-SUPER-MARE, GLOUCESTER, CHELTENHAM, BROMSGROVE, MARLBOROUGH, READING, ETC.; also DAILY FROM BRISTOL TO BOURNE-MOUTH, TORQUAY AND PAIGNTON.

DAILY CONNECTIONS from SALISBURY TO AMESBURY, ANDOVER, TIDWORTH, FORDINGBRIDGE, also DAILY FROM SOUTHAMPTON TO NEW FOREST, WINCHESTER, BASINGSTOKE, ALDERSHOT, GUILDFORD, also DAILY FROM PORTSMOUTH TO PETERSFIELD, CHICHESTER, BOGNOR, WORTHING, BRIGHTON AND EASTBOURNE.

Further Details from **The Terminal Agents**— **THE GREYHOUND MOTORS, Ltd.,** 5, St. Augustine's Place, BRISTOL. ('Phone 24001). **THE OLYMPIC MOTOR SERVICES, Ltd.** 8, Kent Rd., SOUTHSEA.	BOOK HERE :—

10000/28/11/31. G. & M. Organ, Printers, Bristol & Wrington, Somerset.

Timetable of the Olympic Motor Services Ltd Bristol–Southampton service subsequently acquired by Elliott Bros

on the two routes in question and Elliott Bros derived considerable benefit from the extra turnover.

In July 1933 Elliott Bros opened negotiations for the purchase
of Highways Ltd, who had commenced operation on the
London–Plymouth route in March 1928 and who had been
running the following three services since June 1931 : London–
Newquay,   London–Bournemouth–Plymouth/Paignton,   and
London–Ilfracombe. These negotiations were, however, broken
off on 17 August 1933 and eleven days later the Western/
Southern National Companies acquired Highways' business, including goodwill and twenty coaches. Seventeen of these were
Gilfords, recognised as the fastest coaches on the road, and
possessing features that were years ahead of their time, but unfortunately prone to overheating. They were all fitted with 6-
cylinder side valve Lycoming engines of American manufacture.
The transaction was finalised at Exeter on 2 October 1933,
when the Western Area traffic commissioners authorised a licence
for a London–Paignton service to 'Southern National' and a
licence for a London–Plymouth service to 'Western National'.
A 'Southern National' application for excursions and tours from
Bournemouth and for a London–Ilfracombe service, and a
'Western National' application for a London–Newquay service
were withdrawn, following agreement between the National
companies and Elliott Bros on the pooling of receipts. The 1934
timetable leaflets for the routes affected were jointly headed
Royal Blue, Western National and Southern National, and contained the complete operations of both concerns.

The summer of 1933 saw Elliott Bros 'Royal Blue' network at
its peak, with 105 up-to-date long-distance coaches in operation,
all older vehicles having been gradually withdrawn from the
fleet. The following services were running :

A.	Bournemouth–London
B.	Bournemouth–S. Devon–Plymouth London–Bournemouth–S. Devon–Plymouth Folkestone–Brighton–Bournemouth–S. Devon–Plymouth*
C.	London–Salisbury (via Salisbury Plain Camps)
D.	London–Salisbury–Plymouth

E. London–Reading–Bristol–Weston-super-Mare
(Co-ordinated with Greyhound).

F. Bournemouth–Portsmouth
Bournemouth–Margate*

G. Bournemouth–Bath–Bristol
Eastbourne–Southampton–Bath–Bristol*

H. Bournemouth–Weston-super-Mare
Eastbourne–Brighton–Bournemouth–Weston-super-Mare*

J. Bournemouth–Gloucester–Coventry
Portsmouth–Gloucester–Coventry

K. Portsmouth–Birmingham

L. Birmingham–S. Devon–Plymouth

M. Bournemouth–Ilfracombe
Brighton–Bournemouth–Ilfracombe*

N. Birmingham–Ilfracombe

* Co-ordinated with 'Southdown' and 'East Kent'.

Early in 1934 Royal Blue had the distinction of taking delivery of the first AEC 'Q' type vehicle to be put on the road. This revolutionary vehicle represented the first attempt to place the engine other than in the conventional position at the front and was therefore the first full-fronted vehicle. The public reaction was enthusiastic but unfortunately the vehicle had somehow come before its time and nearly twenty years were to elapse before coach engines again left the conventional front position. Four vehicles of this advanced design were bought by Royal Blue and although five more were ordered before the sale of the business to Tillings they did not enter service and presumably the order was cancelled. A print of the 'Q' type coach featured on some of the 1934 Royal Blue timetable leaflets.

Today, when the long-established practice of children's half-fares is being questioned and modified by certain bus companies, it is interesting to note that Royal Blue charged two-thirds for children until the summer of 1934, when the more usual half-fare was adopted.

At this period of the early 30s, all the other interests of the company were continuing successfully. The private-car hire department, equipped with Rolls-Royce and Daimler limousines catered for weddings, dances, theatres, and other social functions,

ROYAL BLUE AUTOMOBILE S

Corfe Castle

Staines Bridge

Devizes Castle

Hungerford

SCALE OF MILES

STOURBRIDGE
HAGLEY
KIDDERMINSTER
HENLEY-IN-ARDEN
BIRMINGH
WORCESTER
STRA
STRATFORD CHURCH
UPTON-ON-SEVERN
EVESHAM
TEWKESBURY
CHELTENHAM
GLOUCESTER
STROUD
CIRENCESTER
CRICKLADE
BRISTOL UNIVERSITY
SWINDO
BRISTOL
CHIPPENHAM
MARLBOROUGH
BATH
BECKHAMPTON
WESTON-SUPER-MARE
BRADFORD-ON-AVON
DEVIZES
TROWBRIDGE
HUNGER
TIDWORTH
WARMINSTER
HEYTESBURY
AMESBURY
BRIDGWATER
TAUNTON
WILTON
SALISBU
LANGPORT
SHAFTESBURY
HURS
ILCHESTER
WIVELISCOMBE
SOUTH MOLTON
ILFRACOMBE
BARNSTAPLE
HAMPTON
WELLINGTON
YEOVIL
SHERBORNE
ROMSEY
RINGWOOD
CULLOMPTON
CHARD
BLANDFORD
WIMBORNE
LYND
DARTMOOR
HONITON
MAIDEN-NEWTON
AXMINSTER
DORCHESTER
EXETER
LYME REGIS
BRIDPORT
WAREHAM
BOURNEMOU
CHRISTCHU
DAWLISH
TEIGNMOUTH
ASHBURTON
BUCKFAST ABBEY
NEWTON ABBOT
TORQUAY
BUCKFASTLEIGH
PLYMOUTH
TOTNES

Royal Blue

VICES ✠ ✠ ✠ A ROUTE MAP

ELLIOTT BROTHERS (Bournemouth) LIMITED

Arundel Castle

Plymouth Hoe

Christchurch Priory

Salisbury

Warwick Castle

Magdalen College Oxford

Leamington

THE CAMERA OXFORD

Lyndhurst

Omnibus Station. Bournemouth.

OXFORD

ABINGDON

WALLINGFORD

MAIDENHEAD

SLOUGH

SUNNINGDALE

STAINES

LONDON

READING

BAGSHOT

KINGSTON

MARGATE

BROADSTAIRS

RAMSGATE

DEAL

DOVER

BASINGSTOKE

GUILDFORD

Guildford Castle

FARNHAM

FOLKESTONE

HYTHE

NEW ROMNEY

ALTON

WINCHESTER

RYE

SOUTHAMPTON

HASTINGS

ARUNDEL

BRIGHTON

SOUTHSEA

CHICHESTER

PORTSMOUTH

WORTHING

NEWHAVEN

SEAFORD

EASTBOURNE

map, 1933

besides being available for long-distance trips for private parties :
a particularly important part of their activities was the late-
night facility offered to theatregoers living in outlying parts of
the Poole/Bournemouth/Christchurch area. Royal Blue excursions and tours from Bournemouth continued to offer a first-rate
service to both residents and visitors. The Isle of Wight tour
was still the most popular excursion from Bournemouth and continued to be operated by Royal Blue coaches based on the
Island. It was the unique practice of Royal Blue to send a
'canvassing coach' round hotels in advance and this service was
backed up by feeder facilities by private car from outlying hotels
to the starting point of the tour. Advertising was of the same
high order and in addition to all the usual media, *The Royal
Blue Weekly* was published, giving details of all the company's
activities—tours to be operated, express service timetables and
private hire facilities.

This useful bulletin was continued for 15 years, from 1919
to 1934, just before the change of ownership occurred. When
Royal Blue sold out in 1935, the lucrative and well organised
excursions and tours passed intact to Hants & Dorset Motor
Services.

ASSOCIATED MOTORWAYS

The most far-reaching development of the 1930-35 period
was the formation of Associated Motorways on 1 July 1934,
after two years of negotiation. It will be seen from the foregoing
that a number of pooling and co-ordination agreements were
entered into following the passing of the 1930 Act, but from
1932 the possibility of a more revolutionary and fundamental
reorganisation was being considered. In the important formative
period, a vital role was played by Elliott Bros, the first significant
step being a meeting at Cheltenham on 8 June, 1932, initiated
by Elliott Bros and sponsored by the Birmingham & Midland
Motor Omnibus Co Ltd ('Midland Red'). This meeting was also
attended by Black & White Motorways and Greyhound, and its
object was to discuss the wider implications of co-ordination,

following a suggestion by the traffic commissioners that the companies should get together in an effort to avoid competing applications and objections. Elliott Bros and Midland Red were in serious opposition on the Birmingham–Oxford–Bournemouth service, an unsatisfactory position which had to be resolved. This first meeting concluded that certain companies, in some areas at least, would have to surrender their individual control over licences if a satisfactory and economic scheme of co-ordination was to be achieved. The next step took place on 11 August 1932, when a meeting between Black & White, Midland Red, Greyhound Motors, and Ribble Motor Services was convened to consider specific co-ordination proposals drawn up by Elliott Bros.

A small committee, consisting of representatives from each company, was formed and after several meetings a report was presented by this committee on 12 September 1933. The report affirmed the belief that the respective companies' groups of express services could be co-ordinated into one complete and workable unit.

The National Companies (Western National and Eastern National) attended a meeting on 26 October 1933, when the co-ordinating parties agreed to protect the stage carriage services of both National Companies: later, Western National became a full member of Associated Motorways through their acquisition of Elliott Bros.

A series of meetings next took place, at which the draft heads of agreement were hammered out, the points of interest being:

1. A specification of the services to be placed in the Pool by each and all the partners.

2. Authority for setting up a Management Committee to control the organisation and operation of the services; also to establish a Control Organisation at Cheltenham, with officers and staff to carry out the directions of the Committee.

3. Authority for licences covering all services in the Pool, to be applied for on behalf of all the companies jointly and

for each licence to be endorsed with the names of the constituent companies.

4. Establishment of a principals' committee, to meet at intervals to consider the current report of the management committee and instruct on policy or give advice on any matters referred to them.

5. Other items relating to costs, booking agencies, apportionment of revenue, opening up of new services, admission of new members, withdrawal from membership, operating schedules and fares.

Applications were submitted to the traffic commissioners in the traffic area concerned and although some 200 objections resulted, the majority were cleared by negotiations prior to the hearings. The hearings were conducted by the then Mr Edwin Herbert, later Sir Edwin, the witness in most of the cases being Mr Preece of Royal Blue. The applications were approved, though some doubt existed in the minds of certain commissioners as to whether each of the companies participating should apply for and be granted separate licences for all the services in the scheme. The applicants contended that this proposal would involve the traffic commissioners in a far more complicated form of control and this argument was accepted. However, the question of the form of licences was again raised by the traffic commissioners in 1936 and a conference was convened between the Metropolitan traffic commissioner and the chairmen of the Western, South Wales, West Midland, and South-eastern traffic areas, together with representatives of the companies. This meeting finalised once and for all the position that only one licence for each service, in the name of all the constituent companies, was necessary.

So came into being in 1934 one of the major co-ordination schemes in the history of road passenger transport in this country, an example of voluntary, sensible, co-operation which is still flourishing and extending to this day. The scheme also represented a most unusual set-up—a partnership of limited liability

companies. The original members of Associated Motorways
were :

> Black & White Motorways Ltd
> Red & White Services Ltd
> Elliott Bros (Bournemouth) Ltd
> Birmingham & Midland Motor Omnibus Co Ltd
> Greyhound Motor Services Ltd
> United Counties Omnibus Co Ltd

As services expanded, these were later joined by Eastern
Counties Omnibus Co Ltd, Lincolnshire Road Car Co Ltd, and
Crosville Motor Services Ltd.

Generally, revenue is allocated in proportion to the percentage
of mileage operated within the pool by each member company.

In the main, the Associated Motorways routes were centred
on Cheltenham, radiating to Swansea, Treherbert, Wolverhamp-
ton, Derby, Nottingham, Kettering, London, Portsmouth,
Bournemouth, and Paignton. Since these early days, additional
routes have been added, the latest being the Yorkshire–Torbay
pool (the 'South West Clipper'), which involves some nine companies in addition to the member companies of Associated
Motorways (1968) and the Newcastle–Torbay service (1969).

Cheltenham therefore became, with London, a focal point for
express road services and it is now possible to travel 'from anywhere to anywhere in Britain via Cheltenham'.

The following are the routes which were transferred by
Elliott Bros to the Associated Motorways organisation in 1934 :

Portsmouth (Southsea)–Birmingham
Portsmouth (Southsea)–Bristol (purchased from Traveller Coaches the
previous year)
Bournemouth–Bristol
Plymouth–Birmingham
Bournemouth/Portsmouth–Coventry
Portsmouth–Bristol via Frome (purchased from 'Olympic' the previous
year)

Elliott Bros' remaining routes were subsequently joined with the
express services of Western/Southern National, to form the new
Royal Blue network which emerged in 1935.

CHAPTER FOUR

THE CONSTITUENT COMPANIES

THE RAILWAY COMPANIES

A S the present 'Royal Blue' system is the result of the fusing of several different lines of development, it is necessary to consider the activities of several other pioneers, including one of our great railways. In the first decade of the twentieth century the Great Western Railway showed great enterprise in deciding to operate a road motor department. This must have been anathema to the many members of the board of directors who were 'dyed in the wool' railwaymen, wielding enormous influence and of great prestige.

Nevertheless, the department was founded and bought what today would appear a weird fleet of vehicles. Solid tyred and chain-driven with flapping canvas hoods, the new vehicles were unleashed on a by no means appreciative farming and hunting community. The passengers mounted the rows of seats by step ladder and the driver's seat exposed him to all the elements.

The GWR's first buses were two 16 hp Canstatt-Daimlers, bought from Sir George Newnes, who had used them on a service between Ilfracombe and Blackmoor Gate as feeders to the Lynton and Barnstaple Railway, but withdrew them after meeting police disapproval of speeds over 8 mph. The GWR used them to open up the Helston–Lizard service on 17 August 1903 and the vehicles, which were 22-seaters, were soon supplemented by additional Milnes-Daimler buses weighing over three tons. Until 1904 a man would have had to walk in front of such a heavy vehicle, so, for the purpose of weighing, some equipment was removed from the bus and subsequently restored.

On 31 October 1903 a Penzance–Marazion service was

opened, and this was followed on 3 April 1904 by a service from Penzance to Land's End. From 1 May 1904 the General Post Office sent their mails by the GWR road motor from Helston, but towards the end of 1904 the Helston–Lizard service was withdrawn because the local council refused to re-metal the road or allow it to be rolled. A further cause of the withdrawal was an accident at Helston depot which resulted in two vehicles being burned out. The depot was closed until mid 1905 when the difficulties with the local authority were resolved and the service resumed. Other services introduced in Cornwall were as follows:

Penzance–St Just, 16 May 1904, with double decked vehicles
Redruth–Portreath, 29 July 1907
St Austell–Bugle, 3 August 1908

In 1905 a depot was opened in Weymouth; and on 26 June of that year a service was introduced between Weymouth and Wyke Regis and lasted until 31 August 1909, when it was withdrawn due to lack of support and the introduction of rail motors on the railway. However, the London and South Western Railway and the GWR collaborated and restarted the Weymouth service on 22 July 1912, using Milnes-Daimler and Maudslay vehicles. The joint GWR/LSWR service between Weymouth and Wyke Regis was the last railway-operated bus service to be introduced and its transfer to The Southern National Omnibus Co Ltd on 1 January 1934 marked the end of railway-owned bus operation.

The vehicles operating from railheads in Cornwall and in the Weymouth area must have been the first regularly timed road services to be resumed following the withdrawal of horse-drawn coaches killed by the railway revolution. It is interesting to speculate as to whether in the more remote areas there was in fact a gap at all. In certain rural districts horse-drawn feeder coaches continued to operate and it is known that three-in-hand coaches were running between Bridport and Crewkerne until 1922. One of the drivers, J. J. Welsh, later became a bus driver with The Southern National Omnibus Co Ltd and, during the summer months, resumed his coaching activities—with a Royal Blue motor coach. The last horse-drawn coach in Cornwall operated in the Bude area until 1919.

WESTERN AND SOUTHERN NATIONAL OMNIBUS COMPANIES

The history of these companies is inevitably bound up in the fortunes of its predecessors and in particular in those of the road motor department of the GWR, the National Steam Car Co Ltd, The National Omnibus and Transport Co Ltd, Thos Tilling Ltd, and The Tilling Group of Companies (The Tilling Association Limited).

It should be mentioned that The National Omnibus and Transport Co Ltd also operated services in the eastern part of England. This Company, which operated under the 'National' fleet name, commenced its south-western area developments in 1919 and depots were opened at Yeovil, Stroud, Taunton, Bridgwater and Trowbridge. To this network were added the services (and in several cases, the premises and vehicles) of operators both large and small whose businesses had been acquired from time to time. On the long-distance express service side the 'National' was early in the field and commenced services as follows:

1927   London–Weymouth (later a Southern National service)
1928   London–Ilfracombe (later a Southern National service)
1928   London–Bude (later a Southern National service)
1928   London–Penzance (later a Western National service)
1928   London–Newquay (later a Western National service)

In August 1928, the main line railway companies (as they were then called) were empowered by Parliament to operate or take interest in road services other than those acting purely as railhead feeders. As a result of these powers they became financially interested in the Western and Southern National Omnibus Companies, which had been formed on 1 January 1929 to take over the operations in the South-west of England previously carried out by The National Omnibus and Transport Co Ltd. The GWR bus services in the West of England were amal-

Page 71 (left) a typical booking agent in the 1930s; *(below)* Richmond Hill booking office, one of several similar establishments set up in Bournemouth

Page 72 (above) Coaches loading at Holdenhurst Road garage, Bournemouth, 1930; *(below)* Omnibus and Coach station, Bournemouth, in 1934, with Elliott Bros coach about to descend the ramp to enter the Royal Blue portion of the station. Note the hackney carriage plates still on the coach

gamated with those of the Western National Omnibus Co Ltd.

The names of the two companies reflect the shareholdings accorded, 'Great Western' having the Western National interest and 'Southern' the Southern National. The areas served by each of the companies were related, as far as possible, to the areas served by the particular railway interest.

On Thursday, 2 April 1931 inter-availability arrangements were introduced by the Great Western and Southern Railways with the express coach services between London and certain places in the South-west served by the 'National' companies. The return portions of road tickets from London issued for these destinations by London Coastal Coaches, and by either Western or Southern National from these places to London, were available for third class return journey by train upon payment of a supplementary fare. This was the first instance of inter-availability of tickets between express road services and rail.

The points included in the arrangement were London and Barnstaple, Bodmin, Falmouth, Ilfracombe, Launceston, Lynton and Lynmouth, Minehead, Newquay, Penzance, St Ives, Taunton, Weymouth, Bideford, Bude, Okehampton, and Swanage.

These inter-availability arrangements lapsed when Royal Blue services ceased to operate during the Second World War, and have not been resumed, largely owing to the great increase in express coach traffic and the difficulty of accommodating casual passengers holding rail return tickets.

TOURIST MOTOR COACHES (SOUTHAMPTON) LIMITED

This is an operator whose importance in the build-up of the present day Royal Blue network is apt to be overlooked. The business had its origin in 1919, when a Mr B. H. Ransom established his coach business at Southampton under the fleet name 'Tourist'; and a limited company was formed later, on 7 November 1927, to acquire the businesses of Ransom's 'Tourist Motor Coaches' and Hiawatha Motor Services. About this time the local char-a-banc owners in Southampton were moved away

E

from a position they had long enjoyed at the West Marlands as a result of its being required for a new civic centre.

At the time of its formation, the Company's registered office was at 171 St Mary's Road, Southampton, but as a result of the move from West Marlands a large house with an acre and a half of grounds was acquired in Grosvenor Square and converted into a café with offices above, while the garden was cleared, suitably surfaced, and floodlighting installed.

Before 1927 Tourist Motor Coaches were operating regular excursions from Southampton to London, which developed into a daily express coach service terminating on the 'Embankment'. By November 1928 there were six departures daily in each direction with an additional service (again in each direction) on Fridays and Saturdays. The route was either via the Great West Road or Guildford and passengers were taken up or set down at Eastleigh, Bishop's Waltham, Winchester, and Basingstoke along the way.

On 4 April 1929 certain timings were extended to and from Bournemouth, and on 15 April 1930 one through journey in each direction was instituted via Bournemouth to Exeter, Torquay and Plymouth. During July and August a Friday night service departed from Southampton for Torquay at midnight, connecting with the 8.45 pm from London to Southampton. In the return direction there was a late departure at 7.30 pm from Torquay to Southampton on Saturdays, but no connection for London. On 1 April 1933 Tourist transferred their London terminal to Samuelson's Coach Station (adjacent to Victoria Coach Station) in Eccleston Place, and by this time the Southampton–London summer timetable contained twelve departures daily in each direction with five extended to Bournemouth, where the terminal was 'the Motor Station, The Square'.

Excursions and tours were an important part of the company's operations and a large selection of day, half-day, and evening excursions were offered. A good liaison was maintained with all the shipping companies and guides and special leaflets were printed in various languages for the benefit of cruise passengers, in particular the Nederland Line and the Rotterdamsche Lloyde.

A number of private cars (Daimlers) were available for private parties, mainly for short tours in the summer season.

An enterprising venture was the introduction on 1 June 1930 of a thrice weekly service between Southampton, Warrington and Liverpool, which by 1933 had been extended to Bournemouth and was operating daily during the month of August.

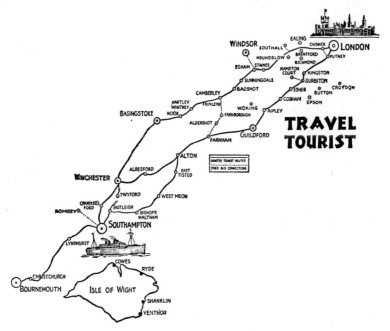

Tourist 'London–Bournemouth' route map reproduced from the block actually used on the Tourist publicity leaflets

The company purchased a specially built fleet of 32-seat Leyland 'Tiger' coaches to work on this long route. This fleet was painted in dark and light blue divided by a cream band around the waist rail. The operation of this service brought offers of purchase from the Southern Railway and the Aldershot & District Traction Co Ltd, both of which were refused, but in November 1934 an offer from Thomas Tilling Limited was accepted.

As a result of this purchase, which was finalised in May 1935, all the express services were transferred to Western National, together with a senior member of the staff who moved to Exeter and remained with the company for many years. On 13 July 1935 the Tourist Services were merged into the Royal Blue network. The local tours from Southampton, and other members of the traffic staff, went to the Hants & Dorset Motor Services Ltd, together with the Grosvenor Square site and the garage in Winchester Road. Twelve of the Tourist vehicles were transferred to 'Western National', twelve to 'Southern National', and twelve to 'Hants & Dorset'. Of the twenty-four vehicles acquired by the National Companies, three were taken into the Royal Blue fleet.

In due course the Western National offered the ex-'Tourist' Liverpool–Southampton–Bournemouth service to Associated Motorways, Royal Blue thereby acting as 'Sellers and Buyers'; and the management committee agreed to accept it. This new arrangement was completed on 1 January 1938, but Royal Blue retained operating control.

GREYHOUND COACHES (WEYMOUTH) LIMITED

This small undertaking was formed on 20 September 1934, following the acquisition by Victory Motors (Weymouth) Ltd (incorporated 20 February 1925) of the local tours business of Greyhound Coaches (Mr R. G. W. Austin), which was founded in 1921. In November 1933 Mr Austin had sold his seasonal Weymouth–Salisbury–London service to The Southern National Omnibus Co Ltd, under whose name the service was resumed on 4 May 1934. The remainder of the business was acquired by Southern National in December 1935 when they bought Greyhound Coaches (Weymouth) Ltd—a business comprising excursions and tours from Weymouth, and a Portland–Portsmouth express service operated mainly for the conveyance of naval ratings.

CHAPTER FIVE

ROYAL BLUE–NATIONAL
1935-1939

SALE OF ELLIOTT BROS

TOWARDS the end of 1934 Elliott Bros decided to sell their business, the obvious purchasers being Thomas Tilling Ltd, who, through their subsidiaries The Western National Omnibus Co Ltd and The Southern National Omnibus Co Ltd, already operated local bus services throughout the four South-western counties, together with substantial express services, particularly since their acquisition of 'Highways' in 1933. Elliott Bros had always maintained very good relations with the National Companies and joint timetables were issued for several services, but they realised they were fighting a losing battle against so large and powerful an organisation and decided to sell while their business was at the peak of its success. An announcement of the transfer was made in December 1934, when the two National Companies deposited applications with the traffic commissioners to take over the express licences of Elliott Bros (Bournemouth) Ltd. The actual date of purchase was 1 January 1935, and National took over the operation of Royal Blue express services on 1 February 1935. The excursions and tours side of the business was transferred to Hants & Dorset Motor Services Ltd of Bournemouth, who thus became freed from the agreement limiting them to the operation of stage carriage services only in the Bournemouth area. 'Hants & Dorset' also took over the Holdenhurst Road garage and the Pavilion garage of Elliott Bros, together with the coaches detailed in Appendix A. The Royal Blue garage at Mill Road, Yarmouth, on the Isle of Wight, was also transferred to 'Hants & Dorset', who continued to carry out the Island Tour with two vehicles and two drivers based at Yarmouth. Later, operations on the Island were maintained by 'Southern Vectis' on behalf of 'Hants & Dorset', though the latter company still holds the licence for the Isle of Wight Tour from Bournemouth. The previous Royal Blue garage is now in the hands of Lakeman and Hayter.

An interesting sidelight on the tour operations generally is that 'Hants & Dorset' continued to use the Royal Blue name and livery for their coaches until the winter of 1936-7 : in fact, several new vehicles arrived in the Hants & Dorset fleet during this period painted in Royal Blue colours. Hants & Dorset were of course just as much entitled to regard themselves as the successors of Royal Blue as Western/Southern National, though the result must have been rather confusing! Similarly, at Southampton, Hants & Dorset retained the coaches they had acquired from 'Tourist' in their old livery until winter 1936-7. No doubt an edict from Tilling's headquarters at the end of 1936 decreed that a rational sorting out was due and that henceforth the name 'Royal Blue' and the distinctive livery should be confined to the express services of Western/Southern National. From this date onward, all Hants & Dorset coaches appeared in green and cream livery, although until 1945 the fleet name continued to be exhibited in oval form, with the words 'Hants & Dorset Motor Services' surrounding the words 'Royal Blue and Tourist', with a buckled belt underneath!

Apart from the remaining vehicles and goodwill, the following property was transferred from Elliott Bros to Western/Southern National:

> *Leasehold*: Lock-up shop, booking office and kiosk at Torquay, Car Park. The half-share in a booking office, previously shared with 'Tourist', at Winchester.
> Lock-up shop, used as booking office, at Paignton.
> Waiting room and booking office at Bristol.
> *Freehold*: Rutland Road Works, Bournemouth.

With the sale of the business Mr J. T. G. Elliott retired but Mr H. H. Elliott, the last of the four-in-hand drivers, began to

look for new interests. Finding his first venture in property invest-
ment too static and undemanding, he bought a farm near
Sturminster Marshall, Dorset, in 1936 and subsequently several
farms in South Africa. However, the outbreak of War in 1939
caused a breakdown of the latter venture with, in Mr Elliott's
words, 'An utter waste of effort, hard work and capital'. The
Dorset farm, on the other hand, progressed from strength to
strength and at the time of writing we are again able to quote
Mr Elliott's own words . . . 'I am very fortunate after a very
high-speed life, to live in a beautiful part of Dorset, surrounded
by a staff of "genuine" people with but one thought—future
progress'; no doubt this attitude explains why Elliott Bros
(Bournemouth) Ltd achieved such success.

What were the immediate results of the changed ownership
of Royal Blue? Firstly, Western and Southern National auto-
matically became partners in Associated Motorways, who were
faced with the problem that, on 31 December 1934, Elliott Bros
had some 30,000 excess miles in the Associated Motorways pool.
The position was cleared by the companies in deficit to the pool
buying the excess miles from Elliott Bros and taking it to their
credit in proportion to their agreed mileage ratios. Secondly,
Thomas Tilling Ltd, through their control of Western/Southern
National and their interest in United Counties became major
partners in Associated Motorways. Perhaps the first innovation
noticeable to the travelling public, arising from the change of
ownership of Royal Blue, was the appearance of new coaches
of 'Bristol' manufacture on the London–Bournemouth service
on 1 March 1935; and it must be mentioned that the Tilling
organisation controlled the 'Bristol' chassis and engine works.
Altogether, twenty-eight 'Bristol' coaches came into the Royal
Blue fleet during 1935. In March 1935 the first timetable leaflet
was issued under the new ownership; this was headed 'The
Southern National Omnibus Co Ltd & The Western National
Omnibus Co Ltd, Proprietors of Royal Blue Services' and
featured the new 'Bristol' coach on the cover. By the summer
of 1935 all the timetable leaflets included the 'Royal Blue'
heading, not excepting those express services which had

previously been owned by Western/Southern National only.

Elliott Bros *Royal Blue Weekly* was replaced by a Royal Blue & Greyhound *Monthly Bulletin*, which was in effect an abbreviated timetable in book form containing all the services, together with a route map and a summary of the alterations or new facilities applicable to that month's issue. Until post-World War II years, Royal Blue never issued a full-scale timetable book; each route was covered by a separate leaflet and the only comprehensive detail was that contained in the Weekly/Monthly Bulletins.

The Royal Blue head office and management were transferred to the Western/Southern National headquarters at 48-50 Queen Street, Exeter, though the vehicle operating centre continued to be at Bournemouth, with an operating superintendent in charge of services at the coach station and an engineering superintendent in charge at Rutland Road garage. Mr C. H. Preece, former traffic manager of Elliott Bros, became traffic superintendent, express services, based at Exeter.

At this time a decision had to be taken which was to have a fundamental effect on the future of express services in the South-west. The issue was whether the seasonal, terminal-to-terminal, type of operation previously carried out by the National Companies was to be the pattern for the future—and from the profitability angle there was much to commend it—or whether the Royal Blue pattern of limited stop, all the year round, service should prevail. The internal battle was intense and at times heated; in the end, however, the Royal Blue pattern carried the day and the South-west thereby gained facilities for intermediate and cross-country travel which have now become vital.

Western/Southern National lost no time in expanding the Royal Blue network and in April 1935 bought the business of A. E. Good (trading as Silver Cars) of Station Road, Seaton, acquiring this operator's licence for a London–Bournemouth–Exmouth service. The acquisition of Tourist, Royal Blue, and Silver Cars in close succession had confronted the National Companies with something of an administrative problem, and they immediately set to work to merge the various services and produce simplified timetables. These proposals were put before the Metropolitan Area traffic commissioner in April 1935 and involved 18 applications, together with the surrender of 8 licences. There was opposition from Shamrock & Rambler Motor Coaches Ltd of Bournemouth, who were concerned at the increased competition from London (Kings Cross Coach Station) to Basingstoke and intermediately to Bournemouth; but the position was cleared by negotiation, Royal Blue agreeing to restrictions on bookings on certain journeys.

REVISED SERVICES

The revised services were approved by the traffic commissioners and it was estimated that they would result in a 50 per cent saving of vehicle journeys and some 1,400 miles per day. Daily departures from London were reduced to seventeen. To the travelling public, the new timetables offered greater simplification, together with improved connections at Bourne-mouth for cross-country services to Kent, Sussex, and Hamp-shire on the one hand and to Devon and Cornwall on the other. In one or two cases facilities were increased (eg to Taunton, Ilfracombe and Minehead). These revised co-ordinated time-tables were brought into operation on 13 July 1935.

It is interesting to note that, from 1935 the former Western/ Southern National express routes were served by the blue coaches, familiar for so many years in the South of England, and indeed a number of National coaches were repainted in the slightly-restyled 'Royal Blue' colours adopted by the National companies as their standard express service livery. Royal Blue coaches were seen in Cornwall for the first time on express services.

With the exception of a few independent operators, of whom the most important were Orange Luxury Coaches (now part of the George Ewer organisation), George Ewer & Co (Grey-Green Coaches), and A. Timpson & Sons, the National Companies had become by 1935 the sole providers of express services between

London and Bournemouth and on the routes linking Somerset, Devon, and Cornwall with London.

In March 1936 a further small addition was made to the Royal Blue network by the acquisition of Scarlet Pimpernel Cars and Motor Supplies Ltd of Ilfracombe. This company, besides their main excursions and tours business, operated a seasonal coach service between London and Ilfracombe, which was merged into the Royal Blue service.

EXPANSION OF FACILITIES

The years 1936 to 1939 were characterised by a steady expansion of facilities, with a keen eye to innovations and new business, all in the best tradition of the former Elliott Bros. By summer 1936, the timetable leaflets had been simplified and the rather ponderous heading containing the full names of both National Companies and 'Proprietors of Royal Blue Services' had been streamlined to just, 'Royal Blue', with the 'flying wheel' which was for so many years the trademark of Western/ Southern National. On 11 July 1936 through running began between Bournemouth and Brighton jointly with Southdown Motor Services.

As part of the Western/Southern National organisation, with its extensive network of local tours from centres in the South-west, Royal Blue was quick to seize the new opportunities this offered and in 1937 instituted their 'Inclusive Holidays in the South & West of England'. These holidays included, in one comprehensive price, travel by Royal Blue between London (or other selected towns) and a seaside resort, full hotel accommodation (all meals and gratuities) for one or two weeks, transport between coach station and hotel, and local coach tours (three tours for one week's stay, or five tours for two weeks' stay). By summer 1938 inclusive holidays of this nature were offered at Bournemouth, Weymouth, Torquay, Ilfracombe, Lynton, Weston-super-Mare, Penzance, Newquay, Seaton, Bath, and Bristol. In those happy days before recurrent financial crises and endless inflation, what did such a holiday cost?

Looking at, say, the Weymouth holiday, and bearing in mind the words of the booklet, 'No attempt has been made to obtain cheap Holidays by reserving inferior accommodation or offering a poor range of tours', the overall price was £6 10s 0d (£6.50) for 8 days or £10 19s 6d (£10.98) for 15 days! There were also three Channel Coast tours, of seven, nine, or fourteen days, using express services for travel all along the South Coast from Margate to Penzance in easy stages, stopping at different hotels en route. The fourteen-day tour was planned 'on a lavish scale', with free days in Margate, Eastbourne, Bournemouth, and Newquay, together with a series of local tours to Land's End, Cheddar Caves, and Exmoor—1,200 miles of travel and all hotel expenses for £16 16s 0d (£16.80).

In 1937, Royal Blue also began the process of extending the network of routes into Cornwall, a process which has continued to the present day; on 10 May in that year the summer feeder service from Okehampton via Tavistock, Liskeard, Lostwithiel, and St Austell to Mevagissey was inaugurated. This service linked at Okehampton with the trunk routes to London, the South Coast, etc. On the same date, one Bournemouth–Taunton journey in each direction was extended via Minehead, Exford, Lynton, and Combe Martin to Ilfracombe, thus enabling this popular North Devon resort to be approached from Taunton either via South Molton and Barnstaple, or by a more scenic route via Minehead and Exmoor.

FIRST ROAD/AIR LINK-UP

A further innovation, and again one which has led to important developments in post-war years, was the introduction of a daily non-stop journey in each direction between London and Bournemouth—the 'Channel Coast Express': this did the journey in 4h 37m, including a 20 minute refreshment break at Hartley Wintney. This compares with the summer 1968 London–Bournemouth non-stop journeys taking 4h 10m, including a 15 minute refreshment break at Winchester. But the most spectacular development of 1937 was the inauguration of the combined Coach/Air service to the Isle of Wight, one of the earliest of such arrangements in Great Britain. The Royal Blue London–Bournemouth service was used to convey passengers to and from Southampton Airport (Eastleigh), where they were transferred with the minimum of delay on to planes of the Portsmouth, Southsea, and Isle of Wight Aviation Ltd, which whisked them in 10 minutes to Ryde Airport. Three journeys per day in each direction were offered, with a fourth during the peak of the season, and the overall journey from London (Victoria) to Ryde Airport was achieved in 4 hours at a cost of 20s 3d (101p) (day return) or 24s (120p) (period return). The 1937 timetable leaflet included a tear-off declaration to be signed by the parent or guardian of any passengers under 21 years of age, giving consent for them to make the air journey, but this was dispensed with in the following year. Air travel in 1937 was not the commonplace which it is today and we find the aircraft company safeguarding its interests in the conditions of carriage :

> In particular the Company reserves the right to exclude from carriage any person under the influence of drink, drugs or narcotic, any person of unsound mind or afflicted with any contagious disease, any person who behaves in an improper manner, or who for any other reason might endanger the safety or comfort of the aircraft or its occupants. Any person excluded under this paragraph shall not be entitled to repayment of the fare paid.

The interests of those on the ground were also protected, '. . . nor must any article be thrown from the aircraft while in flight', and finally passengers were forbidden to walk in front of the aircraft to avoid being chopped up by the propellers! The air service is no longer operated and the most rapid facility London–Isle of Wight (Cowes) that Royal Blue now offers (summer 1968) is 4h 40m via Red Funnel Steamer from South-ampton. So things do not always get faster and faster !

A further extension of facilities in the shape of a new Bridport–Bristol service was refused in May 1937 but was resubmitted a year later in May 1938 and heard by the Western Area traffic commissioners. The application was made by Western/Southern National in conjunction with the Greyhound Express Services

of the Bristol Tramways & Carriage Co Ltd, and was opposed
by the London Midland & Scottish and Southern Railways; it
must be recalled that in these pre-war days when the term
'rationalisation' had not achieved its present meaning the LMS
were involved in the operation of the Somerset & Dorset
Railway from Bristol to Bournemouth. The object of the new
road service was to provide a cross-link between the existing
south coast express services and the Associated Motorways network northward from Bristol; and connections were also planned
at Yeovil with the Exeter–London route, enabling passengers
from East Devon and Dorset to reach Shaftesbury, Salisbury,
Andover etc. It was the first significant attempt by Royal Blue
to build up a completely new cross-country link, a development
which was to become so important and significant twenty-five
years later with the closure of railway lines. The witnesses
supporting the application were mainly town clerks or members
of town or city councils, who gave evidence of the need for the
new service in view of the inferior facilities then available to
passengers making these cross-country trips.

On this occasion the application was granted and the service
began on 1 July 1938: one journey in each direction, making
the trip from Bridport to Bristol in 3 hours via Yeovil, Somerton,
Glastonbury, Wells and Farrington Gurney. In post-war years
the Bridport–Bristol Royal Blue route became incorporated in
the Associated Motorways Exmouth–Bridport–Bristol–Cheltenham service, a logical step. The only other significant
development during 1938 was the deviation of certain journeys
on the London–Bournemouth service via Aldershot, between
Guildford and Farnham.

By 1939 the war-clouds were gathering and events were
moving inexorably towards that holocaust which was to disrupt
the lives of countless millions and put a term to nearly sixty
years of steady development as far as Royal Blue was concerned.
As if to presage coming disaster, Royal Blue operating staff
came out on strike for the first time in the undertaking's history
from May 1 to 14 1939. Nevertheless, even on the brink of the
precipice, several important developments took place during the

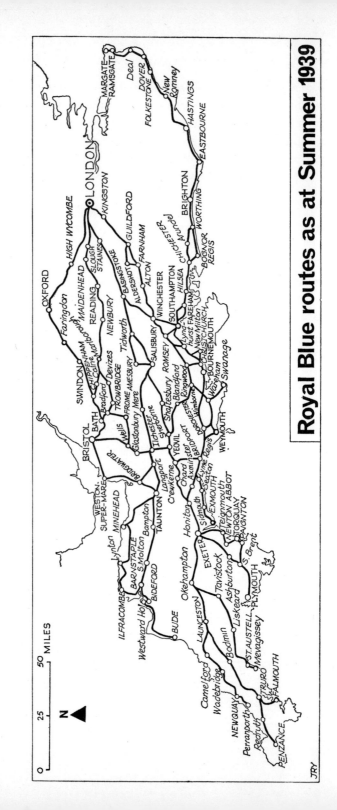

Royal Blue routes as at Summer 1939

last of the pre-war summers. The first of these was the extension of one journey in each direction from Paignton to Brixham and Dartmouth, involving the transport of a Royal Blue coach across the Higher Ferry, Dartmouth. Secondly, a new 'leg' into Cornwall was opened up, from Launceston via Camelford, Wadebridge, and Newquay to Perranporth, with one journey daily in each direction during the summer. Finally, the experiment with non-stop journeys between London and Bournemouth had proved so successful that in the summer of 1939 the following new non-stop facilities were introduced :

1. London–Exeter, the 'Cornish Coast Express'. Saturdays and Sundays only. 8 hours.
2. London–Minehead, the 'Minehead Express'. Saturdays and Sundays only. 8 hours.
3. London–Weymouth, the 'Weymouth Bay Express'. Saturdays and Sundays only. 6h 20m.

The first and third of these reduced the running time by 30-45 minutes compared with normal journeys, but the Minehead Express effected a saving of some 90 minutes.

So, the summer of 1939 found 'Royal Blue' operating the most extensive and comprehensive network in its history. To many of us the outbreak of the World War in September seemed like the end of everything and six and a half harrowing years were to pass before any semblance of normality returned. But the historian is in the privileged position of being able to look forward from any given point in the past, and it can now be seen that during the years 1935 to 1939 were sown the seeds of many developments which came to full fruition in the post-war period, fifteen to twenty years later.

CHAPTER SIX

THE WAR YEARS 1939-1945

THE outbreak of war on 3 September 1939 found the Royal Blue express services carrying considerable holiday traffic, which, during the June–September period normally supplemented the basic all-the-year traffic. The immediate effect of the outbreak of hostilities was a rush of return ticket holders who, with tickets booked for return up to three weeks ahead, all sought to make their way home as soon as possible. Despite the company's standard regulation that at least forty-eight hours' notice of return journey must be given, all passengers presenting themselves for travel were carried, even though this often necessitated hiring additional vehicles.

THE EFFECTS OF WAR

From 1 September 1939 'black-out' regulations were imposed and driving became far more hazardous at night. Numerous difficulties resulted and there was a startling increase in road accidents during the winter months, particularly during December.

Within a short time, traffic booked to travel from London and other large centres became substantial, consisting to a large degree of voluntary evacuees plus the travellers who normally used express road services to reach destinations not readily served by rail. A few vehicles were also used at this time to handle evacuee children and other special traffic from London.

The first timetable changes resulting from war-time con-

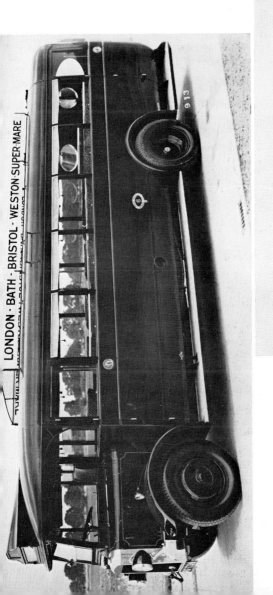

Page 89 (above) Elliott Bros ADC coach with Hall Lewis body, 1928; *(right)* Elliott Bros AEC 'Q' coach, 1934

Page 90 (*top*) Elliott Bros AEG Regal coach with Duple body, 1930; (*centre*) Southern National Leyland TS 2 with Beadle body, 1929, the type used on the 'National' express services of the time; (*below*) Leyland TS 2, 2863 – delivered to Western National in 1929, rebodied by Beadle in 1937 for Royal Blue, and converted to gas-producer operation in the war

ditions came towards the end of September, when all 'pleasure' facilities were deleted—such journeys as were specifically designed to provide day excursions within a 40-50 mile radius of centres like Bournemouth and Torquay. This was followed in October 1939 by special reduced winter timetables to meet the exigencies of fuel rationing, which had been introduced on 22 September. These factors, and the restrictions on the use of private cars arising from petrol rationing, caused traffic to rise considerably above the normal winter level, with a resultant sharp rise in receipts per mile.

During war-time, the conveyance of military personnel was naturally important, especially as Royal Blue served the Salisbury Plain Area and afforded direct facilities to and from Bulford and Tidworth Camps. Shortly before the war, the Bourne-mouth–West of England service had also been diverted to serve Bovington Camp, which could not be reached by rail. Other military and RAF establishments, both large and small, came into being on Royal Blue routes and many modifications were made to cross-country services at the request of the military authorities, to improve facilities for personnel at these camps.

An additional class of traffic, arising from war-time conditions, consisted of parents travelling to see their evacuated children in their new homes; this was usually day-return traffic, mainly on Sundays, but it was nevertheless quite substantial in volume, and of considerable value in preserving morale.

BLITZKRIEG

Summer 1940 saw the disastrous military collapse in France; and the loss of so much equipment led to the requisitioning of a number of the company's vehicles for military purposes. The grim period of the air war then commenced, with London bombed nightly from 7 September to 13 November and attacks continuing for the remainder of 1940 and on into 1941. With its network of routes from London across southern and south-western England, it is not surprising that Royal Blue vehicles became directly involved in the aerial warfare.

F

The Southern National's first experience of bombardment came in August 1940, when the roof of Portland garage was damaged by bomb blast. This was followed in October 1940 by a more tragic incident, when the Weymouth garage received a direct hit, resulting in the death of four men, many injuries, and severe damage to fourteen vehicles, including former Royal Blue coach 3732 (LJ 1529, AEC Regal), later repaired. In November, two Southern National vehicles on hire to the military at Houndstone Camp near Yeovil were completely destroyed by bombing. The fantastic and unparalleled conditions under which public service vehicles were operated at this period can best be brought to life by one or two personal anecdotes. In the simple, stark words of the driver of the 3.30 pm Bournemouth–London coach on 7 November 1940 :

> I now come to a night I shall never forget. I left Bournemouth at 3.30 pm and had not got far before it was black-out time. It was a lovely night with a full moon which illuminated the countryside almost like daylight.
> I had an excellent journey and was nearing Aldershot when the sirens sounded the alert. I could see as I approached London that they were 'having it'. After passing through Cobham and Esher, I could clearly see from the flashes of gunfire and bursting bombs that a serious raid was in progress. Soon a red glow began to appear and as we got nearer London this seemed to fill my whole horizon. I passed through Kingston and had hardly got clear when things began to happen in real earnest. Anti-aircraft guns began firing from unseen positions beside the road and mingled with their firing were the explosions of falling bombs. I thought the only thing to do was to keep going and hope for the best. I was actually on Putney Heath when there was a terrific explosion and the coach seemed to shoot away from under me. I felt as though I was flying through the air with the coach: I clung on to the steering wheel although this did not stop me from being severely bumped around inside the cab. I found myself rushing towards some trees, then the coach swerved and hit a fence and wall. As soon as I recovered my senses I rushed round to the passengers and found them shaken but unharmed. Fifty yards back down the road a huge crater showed where a bomb had fallen just behind us as we passed.

The driver was taken to hospital suffering from shock and bruising. Fortunately no passengers were badly hurt and they were able to disperse to their destinations by local transport; the coach, not seriously damaged, was taken on to Victoria Coach Station.

This type of dilemma, 'to shelter or not to shelter', often faced drivers; the passengers' attitude nearly always was, 'leave it to you, driver—get through if you can'.

Another eye-witness account relates to Southampton on 1 December 1940 and again in the words of the driver:

> I was driving the 4.30 pm London–Bournemouth service, scheduled to call at Southampton. On arrival at Farnham (some forty miles from the port) I noticed a bright red glow in the sky, away in the direction of the coast. On arrival at Winchester I was told that Southampton was being raided. I carried on and on the outskirts of the town the police stopped me and advised me about a diversion. I eventually got to Bassett Cross, where I set down several passengers. At this time anti-aircraft guns were firing. From this point at the top of the common one looked right over Southampton, which seemed to be a mass of flames. The remaining passengers asked if I was going any further: I said I would try and turned down the avenue towards the town. I got nearly to the Coach Station when I was again stopped by the police, who wanted to know where I was going. I said, 'To the coach station'. They said it was impossible to get through owing to debris and the danger from falling buildings. I realised the truth of this for, as we were speaking, I saw the whole front of a large building slowly lean over and then, with increasing speed, crash to the roadway where it disintegrated in dust and flame. Shops and houses were blazing on both sides of the road.

After making a suitable deviation, this coach was able to continue on its journey to Bournemouth.

Following the fall of France to the German forces, the threat of invasion across the Channel had become very real. The form it might take could only be guessed at, with the result that precautions had to be taken against airborne landings as well as coastal landings. Huge concrete and steel barriers were erected across roads, leaving only an easily-sealed 'gate' through which traffic could pass. Many of these roadblocks were manned and it was quite common for Royal Blue coaches to be stopped by armed soldiers and the passengers' identity cards inspected. It must also be recalled that, to give as little assistance as possible to any invading army, all signposts and other direction signs had been removed from roads.

Each stage of the war had its particular effect on public transport. The heavy air-raids on London and the industrial centres, particularly during the closing months of 1940, caused waves of evacuees, and Royal Blue had to contend with long periods of traffic at 'Bank Holiday' level. People who had been bombed out of their homes arrived at Victoria Coach Station with their remaining belongings tied up as best they could; sometimes a bundle of bedding, sometimes a broken suitcase, or even a bird in a cage or a domestic pet. Tragic little groups were to be seen 'camping out' in the vestibule or booking hall, waiting patiently for the first available seat to anywhere away from the noise, danger, and ugliness of London at war.

On 12 March 1941, the Royal Blue depot at Bournemouth received some damage from a high-explosive bomb.

Excluding London, Plymouth had the unhappy record of being the second most-bombed town in Great Britain and on four separate occasions damage was sustained to vehicles and premises at the Western National Laira Bridge Road Garage. On the first of these occasions, 21 March 1941, twenty-four vehicles were damaged, including nine which were a total loss; the twenty-four included two Royal Blue AEC Regal coaches, which only received relatively minor 'wounds' and were subsequently repaired. No Royal Blue vehicles were involved in the subsequent three raids which damaged the Plymouth garage.

On 16 April 1941, a heavy attack on London caused great destruction in the area around Victoria Coach Station and nineteen Royal Blue vehicles were damaged when a shower of incendiary bombs fell close to them. It is a remarkable tribute to the spirit of the staff that despite the damage, every service was operating next day, albeit with shattered windows patched up with destination blinds and other makeshift repairs. Mr Preece was staying in a hotel near the Coach Station on this night and he describes his experiences as follows:

A furniture warehouse near the river had caught fire and enemy dive-bombers were endeavouring to spread the conflagration. I could see the front of the coach station above the intervening buildings, shining with a luminous pink light from surrounding fires. I made my way to the coach station in rushes, taking whatever cover was available when I heard the whistle of bombs.

At the station I collected some of our drivers, so that we would be ready to get the vehicles out if fire started from the thousands of burning embers that rained about us. We were looking towards the worst of the fires when we saw a parachute descending: it was silhouetted against the glare and appeared to be supporting a man. Thinking it was a shot-down enemy pilot, we started to cheer. As it descended we could hear the clang of fire engines racing towards the fire from several different directions. The parachute had just disappeared behind intervening build-ings when there was a most appalling explosion. A great mushroom of debris and dust arose from where a parachute-mine had exploded. The great cloud blotted out the fire which tinged its edges with orange light, creating a nightmare picture of destruction. In the silence which followed, we wondered what had happened to the firemen—the bells were still.

The railways were experiencing great physical difficulties from air-raid damage, particularly in London, where so many main lines are on viaducts and embankments. Road damage was less troublesome, as traffic could find a way round almost any incident. The GPO suffered great destruction to postal and other vital communication centres, but the authorities in the South-west showed great ingenuity in surmounting difficulties. For a brief period Royal Blue carried packets of HM telegrams between Portsmouth, Southampton, and Bournemouth.

GAS PRODUCERS

As the gravity of the war increased, so the two great pressures of fuel shortage and the demand for increasing passenger accommodation squeezed the management in their relentless grip. The staff were working under great strain; only those who have driven in black-out conditions can fully appreciate what was entailed in handling a large passenger vehicle over long distances with only a glimmer of light. There was the ever-present risk of plunging into a bomb crater, or over a collapsed bridge; and the chance of failing to see the dim red light per-mitted by war-time regulations on some stationary vehicle. For the imaginative driver there was also the realisation that if a parachute landing were attempted, the first and only warning might be a burst of machine-gun fire from the dark roadside.

To combat the growing fuel shortage, gas producers were purchased and attached to a number of Royal Blue coaches during the summer of 1942. Altogether seventeen Bristol JJW and eight Leyland TS2 coaches were converted to gas operation,

Tilling type 2T2 Producer Gas trailers being employed: the conversion work was carried out at the Western National Taunton depot, which became the main centre for the company's gas producer activities. These gas trailers were, in effect, small anthracite burners which produced combustible gas for feeding into the induction pipe of the vehicle engine. Despite great technical ingenuity these machines could only produce a low-efficiency fuel, while they suffered from many defects, usually connected with the fire which had to be maintained at exactly the correct size and temperature.

To most people, a fire and a motor vehicle were two things to be kept severely apart, yet here were coaches moving along the road towing a weird contraption with a fire in its belly! Another serious drawback was the damage to valves and combustion chamber caused by the gas fuel, which gave an effective engine life of only 50,000 miles.

ROYAL BLUE CEASES OPERATIONS

In May 1942 the so-called 'Baedaeker raids' on cathedral cities took place, including a severe fire and delayed-action bombing raid on Exeter, where the Royal Blue headquarters were situated. The offices luckily escaped damage, though several members of the staff lost their homes. Owing to the amount of debris in the city's streets and the danger from unexploded bombs, the Royal Blue services were diverted round Exeter by-pass and a vehicle which had been laying over in Exeter was used to provide a feeder service between the coach station and the by-pass. The driver was an official of the company, and passengers had to lie down on the floor to minimise the risk from flying glass from delayed explosions. Practically every journey had to use a different route through the city streets owing to the discovery of further unexploded bombs.

Finally, in October and November 1942 came that sad day when, as a result of the grave fuel situation, all Royal Blue Express Services had to cease, after having served the South-west generally and in particular London, Southampton, Portsmouth, Bristol, and Plymouth during the height of the air-raids. The last Royal Blue coach left London, Victoria Coach Station, on 17 October. This was an AEC Regal working the 5.45 pm to Basingstoke, Andover, and Salisbury; and for the first time in over fifteen years, a day dawned without a coach on the London–Salisbury–Plymouth highway.

The war as it affected passenger transport had taken a new turn and no one could foretell whether the familiar blue coaches would ever resume their pre-war role. Some of the vehicles were hired for military purposes and others were used for the remainder of the war to supplement local works and factory services. The achievements of Royal Blue during the first three years of war, apart from the maintenance of normal services, may be summarised as follows :

Evacuation of London
    (a) Number of vehicles used   103
    (b) Number of passengers carried   27,830
    (c) Number of miles travelled   22,865
    (d) Number of separate occasions
        on which vehicles turned out   931

Invasion Stand-by from Western/Southern National Coach Fleets
    (a) Number of drivers   134
    (b) Number of vehicles held against
        War Department requirements   134

The table on page 98 illustrates the gradual running-down of the regular Royal Blue services from September 1939 to the cessation of operations in November 1942. The table also shows that there was limited resumption of increased summer facilities on trunk routes during 1940 and again, to a diminished extent, during 1941; thereafter the picture is one of steady with-drawal until the express services ceased.

JOURNEYS PER WEEK IN EACH DIRECTION

	Peak Summer 1939‡	Winter 1939-40 (9 October)	Summer 1940 (1 June)	Winter 1940-41 (30 September)	Summer 1941 (26 July)	Winter 1941-2 (29 September)	Summer 1942	Winter 1942 (1 September)
London–Bournemouth	84	42	42	42	42	42; reduced to 31 on 3 Nov	31: reduced to 25 on 5 August	24
Bournemouth–Plymouth	36	14	21**	14	14	14	14	14
London–Plymouth	23	7	14	7	14	7	7	7
Bournemouth–Portsmouth*	49	29	31	29	29	28	28	28
Bournemouth–Ilfracombe	14	7	14	7	7	7	7	7
London–Salisbury (Local)	7	7	7	7	7	7	7	7
London–Ilfracombe	4	Suspended 11 September 1939 for duration of war.						
Bournemouth–Weston-super-Mare	14	1: Bournemouth–Taunton only	1: B'mouth–Taunton 1††; 7: Taunton–Weston	1: Bournemouth–Taunton 1††	1††	1††	1††	1††
London–Bournemouth–Exmouth	7	0	7: Bournemouth–Exmouth only	Suspended 29 September 1940 for duration of war.				
Exeter–Penzance	7	0	7	7	7	Suspended 29 September 1941 for duration of war.		
Exeter–Mevagissey	7	0	4	Suspended 29 September 1940 for duration of war.				
Exeter–Dartmouth	7	Suspended 18 September 1939 for duration of war.						
Launceston–Newquay–Perranporth	7	0	7	Suspended 29 September 1940 for duration of war.				
Barnstaple–Bude	2	Suspended 18 September 1939 for duration of war.						
Southampton–Park Prewett Hospital	2	2	2	Suspended 11 Sept 1940 but resumed 26 Feb 1941 — 2	2	2	2	2
Wareham–Swanage	7	7	7	Suspended 6 July 1940 for duration of war.				
†London–Bristol–Weston-super-Mare	35	9	9	9	Suspended 31 July 1941 for duration of war.			
†Marlborough–Wells	14	7	7	7	Suspended 31 July 1941 for duration of war.			
†Bristol–Bridport–Sidmouth	10	Suspended 18 September 1939 for duration of war.						

‡ Included seven Bournemouth–Dartmouth journeys, replacing suspended Exeter–Dartmouth service.
* Through working to Margate (Joint with 'Southdown' & 'East Kent') ceased on 4 September 1939 for duration of war.
** On 10, 11 and 18 September piece-meal deletions of non-essential journeys took place.
† Joint services with Bristol Tramways & Carriage Co Ltd.
†† Bournemouth–Taunton only.

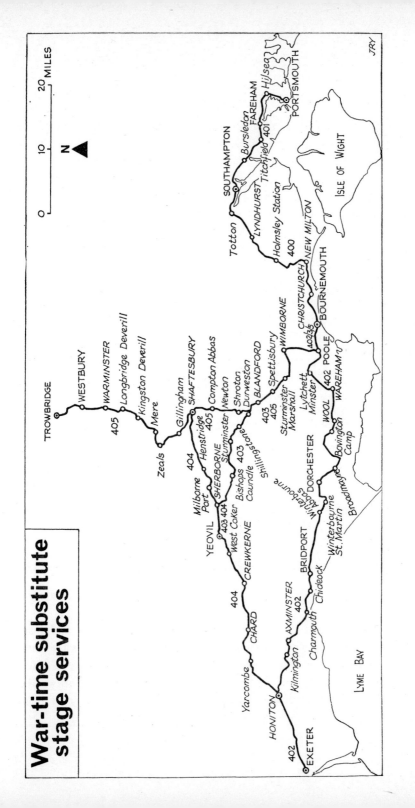

War-time substitute
stage services

TROWBRIDGE

WESTBURY

WARMINSTER

405 Longbridge Deverill

Kingston Deverill

Mere

Zeals

Gillingham

SHAFTESBURY

Compton Abbas

404 Henstridge 405

Milborne Port

Shroton

Newton

SHERBORNE Sturminster

403 404

403 West Coker Bishops

YEOVIL 403 Caundle

Shillingstone

404 CREWKERNE

Sturminster Marshall

BLANDFORD

405 Spettisbury

WIMBORNE

Lytchett Minster

POOLE

402 WAREHAM

WOOL Bovington Camp

Broadmayne

Winterbourne St. Martin

DORCHESTER

Winterbourne Abbas

BRIDPORT

AXMINSTER 402

CHARD

404 Yarcombe

HONITON

Kilmington

Charmouth

Chideock

EXETER

402

WINCHESTER

SOUTHAMPTON

Totton

LYNDHURST

Holmsley Station

400

NEW MILTON

BOURNEMOUTH

CHRISTCHURCH

402/3/5

Bursledon

FAREHAM

Titchfield 401

Hilsea

PORTSMOUTH

ISLE OF WIGHT

LYME BAY

20 MILES

N

0 10

JRY

EMERGENCY REPLACEMENT BUS SERVICES

Nevertheless, November 1942 was not quite 'the end of the road' so far as Royal Blue war-time operations were concerned. In spite of the gravity of the national situation, representations were made to the ministry that there were certain cross-country sections of route which were not covered by ordinary bus services or by suitable railway facilities. The Ministry of Transport officials, living as they did in London with its trunk rail network to all parts of the country, were very hard to convince, but after numerous interviews, backed by pressure from the licensing authority (the wartime designation of the traffic commissioners), the position was at last realised and the following supplementary services were authorised.

> *Service* 400: Bournemouth–Southampton. Four journeys each way. Running time, 88 mins. Vehicles required to work service: two (with *Service* 401).
>
> *Service* 401: Southampton–Portsmouth. Four journeys each way. Running time, 62 mins. Vehicles required to work service: interworked with *Service* 400.
>
> *Service* 402: Bournemouth–Dorchester–Bridport–Honiton–Exeter. Two journeys each way. Running time, 250 mins. Vehicles required to work service: three (interworked with Southern National *Service* 47 Weymouth–Exeter).
>
> *Service* 403: Bournemouth–Blandford–Sherborne–Yeovil. One journey each way. Running time, 136 mins. Vehicles required to work service: one.
>
> *Service* 404: Honiton–Chard–Yeovil–Shaftesbury. One journey each way plus one 'short' working each way Chard–Honiton. Running time, 167 mins. Vehicles required to work service: one.
>
> *Service* 405: Bournemouth–Blandford–Shaftesbury–Warminster–Trowbridge. Two journeys each way. Running time, 215 mins. Vehicles required to work service: two.

All these services were operated daily (weekdays and Sundays).

Service 402 was designed to connect at Exeter to and from Plymouth; *Service* 403 afforded connections at Yeovil to and from Taunton and Crewkerne; *Service* 404 connected at Shaftesbury with 'Wilts & Dorset' services to and from Salisbury; and *Service* 405 afforded connections at Trowbridge to and from Chippenham, Frome, Devizes and Bradford-on-Avon.

Although authorised as stage services and carrying conductors, these routes were partially operated on a limited-stop basis and were maintained by Royal Blue coaches. By this tenuous link, the name of Royal Blue remained in being and the services

One of the tickets specially printed for the war-time emergency services

continued to afford a vital link in the transport pattern of the South-west.

An interesting technical point lay in the fact that *Service* 402 was licensed as two separate services (402 Exeter–Dorchester and 402A Dorchester–Bournemouth) to avoid any semblance of a through express service. The vehicles operated through and the timetable was shown as a through facility but it was necessary for passengers travelling across Dorchester to rebook at that point, as the faretable was in two separate sections.

With cross-country traffic concentrated on these skeleton services at a time of severe petrol rationing, conditions were extremely arduous. One of the authors had the experience on a Saturday in May 1943 of conducting *Service* 402 from Exeter to Bournemouth, owing to a last-minute shortage of operating staff. The vehicle, an AEC Regal, had a full seating load and twenty standing passengers: the fare range was so great that three racks of bell-punch tickets had to be carried and the difficulty of fighting through the moving vehicle, collecting fares, and issuing a selection from so many tickets can well be imagined. Suffice to say, Bridport was almost reached before all the fares were taken. The strain on vehicles of such conditions on hilly roads was also considerable and on the way back from Bournemouth to Exeter, it was 'all out and push' up Chideock Hill! Services of such length, with such high fare ranges, presented quite a ticket problem as, with the best will in the world, it was not possible for conductors to carry bell-punch tickets of every fare denomination. This difficulty was overcome by having special 12/- (60p) part-fare tickets, which could be combined with tickets of lower denominations to produce the fare required.

Apart from minor adjustments to running times and departure times, there were only two significant alterations to the replacement stage services during their three and a half years of operation, viz:

> *Service* 403: from May 1943 onward, a second journey was introduced in each direction between Bournemouth and Yeovil.
> *Services* 400 & 401: from May 1945 these two routes were combined into one through service (400) Bournemouth–Southampton–Portsmouth, four journeys per day, running time 151 mins.

The subsequent history of *Service* 405 Bournemouth–Trowbridge is quite interesting, since it replaced in effect an Associated Motorways facility and not a Royal Blue express service. Even when Royal Blue operations were resumed in April 1946, *Service* 405 continued in fragmented form, ie:

405. Bournemouth–Shaftesbury. Two journeys daily. Running time, 129 mins.

405A. Shaftesbury–Trowbridge. Two journeys daily. Running time, 105 mins.

This persisted until early in 1949, when the Bournemouth–Shaftesbury section ceased and 405A became a normal Western National stage service.

With the cessation of the war in Europe on 8 May 1945 and the dramatic end to hostilities in the Far East in August 1945, thoughts immediately turned to the restarting of express services. The problems were appallingly difficult. Fuel and manpower were extremely restricted until the restocking of the nation's fuel resources, and the release of manpower from the armed forces, had at least commenced. The recovery of vehicles in sadly battered condition from the military and their rehabilitation had to be undertaken, owing to the inability of plants and factories still geared to war needs to make new vehicles. Royal Blue vehicles had come through the war with only one total loss—this was 3631, damaged beyond repair on 11 August 1943. Quite apart from the physical difficulties, many people in high places, used to car transport, did not fully realise the value of express coach services in providing cross-country links and enabling both residents and visitors without cars to see the towns and countryside of England. A former chairman of the company, encountering Mr Preece on the stairs during a visit said, 'We shall never see Royal Blue back again', softening the comment by adding that nevertheless there would always be a job for him.

Subsequent chapters will show what the future in fact held in store.

CHAPTER SEVEN

THE POST-WAR RECONSTRUCTION OF SERVICES 1946-1949

ALTHOUGH the War only finished finally in August 1945, so great is the potential for recovery in human affairs and so strong the urge to push onward to new things that, despite the scars, the difficulties and depletion of resources, before September was out the Minister of War Transport had issued a statement:

> He has therefore now given the Regional Transport Commissioners discretion to allow operators to resume the operation of Express Services provided the applicants can satisfy the Commissioners that (a) the applicants have the necessary vehicles, labour etc etc (b) the Services will not involve any demand on the Ministry of Labour etc etc.

Royal Blue lost no time in responding to this announcement, recognising that several months must elapse in negotiations and determination of applications. It was naturally hoped that during these months the somewhat battered fleet of coaches could be reassembled and refurbished and sufficient staff demobilised to man them. On 13 October Mr Preece wrote to the regional transport commissioner, Sir Alfred Robinson, seeking an interview to discuss the resumption of services and the submission of appropriate applications. The meeting took place in Bristol on 26 October; Sir Henry Piggott, the regional transport commissioner for the Southern area was also present, as were two representatives holding a 'watching brief' for Associated Motorways.

The main points arising from this meeting were that express

services should be recommenced in four progressive stages, that the railways must be consulted in advance, that essential transport connected with prisoners of war or county agricultural committees must not be jeopardised by the more attractive express operations, and that the question of fares must be gone into with great care. The latter was a very difficult consideration : express services had not functioned for three years, the entire fleet was in urgent need of replacement, future prospects were quite unknown at this juncture, competition with the railways had to be taken into account—what was a reasonable level for fares in all these circumstances? The regional fares committees were again functioning and a meeting on 3 October had agreed to leave the question to the central fares committee. Four days later the company confirmed the points discussed at the meeting and outlined their proposals for stage 1, to be introduced on 3 December 1945. The next step was a meeting at Paddington on 26 November with representatives of the Great Western and Southern Railways, and though the minutes are lengthy and hedged with provisos, in effect the railways agreed not to oppose, 'provided it was made clear that this decision was not deemed to represent approval or support of the proposals'! Even as the meeting was in progress came news that the Metropolitan commissioner would not agree to express services in or out of London before 1 February 1946. In view of this setback and the fact that the fares position was still unresolved, the Company agreed early in December to defer the introduction of services until 1 February. Fares did indeed become the main stumbling block and caused a further postponement to 1 April 1946.

Meanwhile the commissioners for the Eastern, Metropolitan, Southern, South-western, West Midland and South-eastern areas all met together in London on 5 February and decided not to accept a proposal by the central fares committee to revise fares on a more uniform mileage basis, involving increases of 20-25 per cent over pre-war level. A proposal by Sir Henry Piggott that there should be a flat 16⅔ per cent increase on all pre-war fares was agreed upon, as this was the amount by which railway fares had increased since the outbreak of war. The way was now open for the applications to be heard but in view of the lapse of time, Royal Blue decided to omit stage 1 of the proposals and proceed initially with stage 2, which in any event had been scheduled for introduction at Easter 1946. Amending applications were deposited on 15 February 1946 and the long-awaited hearing took place in Bristol on 20 February. The services were granted but the decision on fares was deferred in view of representations by the railways that the proposed coach fares should be brought up to a rate comparable with that for rail travel. However, at last the commissioners ruled that $16\frac{2}{3}$ per cent over pre-war level was the acceptable figure and on 15 April the same blue coaches which had ceased in November 1942 started once more on their familiar routes—literally the same coaches, as there had been no fleet renewals at all during war-time and the chassis and body builders had still not switched over from armaments to vehicle manufacture. The services operated were as follows:

London–Bournemouth	:	6 per day.
Bournemouth–Plymouth	:	1 per day plus 1 Bournemouth–Totnes.
London–Plymouth	:	1 per day plus 1 London–Salisbury and 1 Salisbury–Exeter.
London–Bristol	:	2 per day plus 1 Marlborough–Wells.
Bournemouth–Portsmouth	:	4 per day plus Saturday and Sunday only journeys.
Bournemouth–Ilfracombe	:	2 per day plus 1 Bournemouth–Taunton.
Bournemouth–Trowbridge	:	2 per day (continuation of the war-time stage substitute service 405).

Royal Blue was quicker off the mark than most express operators, due largely to the fortunes of war which had only destroyed one vehicle and had not involved the requisitioning of the entire fleet, as happened to some less fortunate operators. So the pre-war Bristols, Leyland Tigers and AEC Regals were back on their old duties and formed the mainstay of the express fleet for some two years, at a time of restricted services and very heavy loadings.

Associated Motorways were not far behind and on 3 June 1946, they too started skeleton services of one journey in each direction on twenty-six of their pre-war routes; and the same day also marked the beginning of stage 3 of Royal Blue's resurgence, with the following additional services:

Page 107 (top) A Bristol JJW coach bought by wnoc Ltd for Royal Blue after its acquisition in 1935; *(centre)* pre-war view of 3631 at Brixham. This former Elliott Bros coach was rebodied by Beadle (as shown) in 1939, severely damaged by enemy action on 11 August 1943, and subsequently broken up; *(below)* Leyland coach passing through war-damaged area of Southampton

Page 108 (*top*) Royal Blue coaches engaged on military manoeuvres during the 'Phoney War', 1940; (*centre*) a Royal Blue coach approaches a military checkpoint; (*below*) war-time departure from Victoria Coach Station, London

London–Bournemouth : 1 extra journey daily in each direction.
London–Plymouth : 1 extra journey daily in each direction, London–Paignton–Dartmouth.
Bournemouth–Trowbridge : taken out of Royal Blue timetable and continued as stage service in Southern National 'Somerset & Dorset Area' timetable.
London–Ilfracombe : service of 2 journeys daily in each direction resumed after 7 years (one via Minehead and one via Barnstaple).
London–Penzance : service of 1 journey daily in each direction resumed after 5 years.

These two or three post-war years were the halcyon days of the South-west. Freed from the anxieties of war but still with many of its restrictions, people wished only to settle down and enjoy that blissful dream—a carefree holiday. Petrol and food were severely rationed and practically everyone travelled by coach or train. The west-country lanes and villages were not cluttered with motor cars, blasted by transistor radios, or spread with litter; and the few who knew where to look could find farms dispensing those unheard-of luxuries—Devonshire cream and home-brewed cider (better than the best champagne).

For the winter of 1946–7, the London–Penzance and London–Dartmouth services ceased as they had always been 'summer only' facilities, but there were two small innovations in the gradual rebuilding of Express facilities:

1. On the London–Bristol route, the Marlborough–Wells connecting journeys were extended through to Weston-super-Mare via Cheddar.
2. The South Coast Express began to re-appear in embryo form by the inclusion of Portsmouth–Brighton–Hastings connections on the Bournemouth–Portsmouth service.

The Summer 1947 timetable was introduced on 19 May (Whitsun) and marked stage 4 of the resumption of Royal Blue services. The innovations were:

London–Bournemouth: an extra journey in each direction daily, making 8 in all and including the resumption of the 11.30 pm night coach from London to Bournemouth (daily to Southampton, arriving 2.55 am; Fris, Sats and Suns only to Bournemouth, arriving 4.7 am).
Bournemouth–Plymouth: 1 extra journey per day in each direction.
London–Plymouth: London–Dartmouth journeys resumed and Salisbury–Exeter journeys extended to Paignton.

G

London–Bristol: increased to 4 journeys per day, plus the Marlborough–
Weston-super-Mare feeder service. The 4 journeys included the resumption of the London–Oxford–Swindon–Bristol route (1 in each direction).

Bournemouth–Portsmouth: increased to 7 journeys per day, with connections on the Coastal Express, Portsmouth–Margate.

The London–Penzance service reappeared on the same basis
as Summer 1946 and the Bournemouth–Park Prewett Hospital
facility was resumed on Weds and Suns after 5 years.

The Winter 1947-8 timetable, introduced on 13 October,
reverted to that in operation the previous winter with one
important difference—through running recommenced on the
South Coast Express between Bournemouth and Brighton with
two journeys daily in each direction.

So, by the end of 1947 the skeleton around which the present
Royal Blue network was built was established.

The year 1948 was marked by two important developments.
First, in May there was the initial post-war delivery of new
vehicles, when 'Bristol' L6B, 27 ft 6 in x 7 ft 6 in, 31-seater
coaches were taken into the fleet; between then and September
1949, forty-five of these new vehicles were acquired (Nos 1200–
1244). Staggered seating and tasteful interior decoration made
these coaches a credit to Royal Blue and its new owners. 'New
owners', because the second important event of 1948 was the
sale of the Tilling group of companies to the British Transport
Commission, who had already earlier in the year taken over the
shares held by the railways in omnibus companies throughout
Great Britain. As a result, Western/Southern National and
Royal Blue became, in effect, nationalised, and it must be said
that this was the happiest example (perhaps the only happy
example!) of post-war nationalisation of industries. All the bus
interests acquired by the British Transport Commission retained
their Company identity and Management; Tillings, the previous
owners, were in effect appointed agents to operate the undertakings on behalf of the British Transport Commission. Each
company continued to manage its own affairs and was looked
upon as a separate financial entity and the only difference was
that the final profit (or loss) went to the government instead of

the Tilling shareholders. By this means flexibility was retained, local interests and considerations were not over-ruled and the dangers inherent in monolithic structures were avoided—over-centralisation, depersonalisation, lack of a sense of responsibility.

But 1948 was a busy year in other ways. On the vehicle side, the work of rebodying the 1937 fleet of AEC Regals was begun in November. The Summer timetable for 1948 also continued the process of building-up and extending services, though there was one deletion—the night coach at 11.30 pm from London to Bournemouth; night travel was still not acceptable in these immediate post-war years and another three years were to pass before a dramatic change occurred. The Bournemouth–Portsmouth service was increased to nine journeys per day, including two through coaches on the South Coast Express to and from Brighton and Margate. The year 1948 also saw the first reappearance of the non-stop journeys, which were to play an important part in the ensuing twenty years: the first was a London–Bude journey, and vice versa, on Saturdays and Sundays only, first stop Taunton, apart from a refreshment break at Hartley Wintney; the London–Taunton section of 150 miles was done in 6h 40m (including 30m at Hartley Wintney). This summer also marked the reintroduction of the London–Exmouth service after eight years—one journey per day, with a Bournemouth–Swanage 'feeder' service on Saturdays and Sundays. The London–Penzance service was back again for the summer, with the addition of a new daily feeder service Exeter–Launceston–Wadebridge–Newquay. Finally, the Bournemouth–Ilfracombe service operated as the previous summer but included a new connection of two journeys per day between Taunton and Weston-super-Mare.

Winter 1948-9 showed very little difference from the previous winter, except that in response to requests the night coach from London to Bournemouth was restored on Wednesdays and Saturdays only, 11.0 pm from London. A London–Bournemouth–Plymouth composite timetable was also produced, but it was in effect a summary of connecting facilities and included no actual through running.

The Summer timetable for 1949 included a number of important additions and the 36-page booklet for this period looked very different from the slim 19-page volume of April 1946. The significant changes were:

London–Bournemouth: increased to 10 journeys daily, including the daily resumption of the night coach, now advanced to 10.30 pm ex-London. Also included were 2 non-stop journeys in each direction, doing the journey in 4h 35m, including 20m refreshment halt at Hartley Wintney, 2m less than in 1937! One journey in each direction was given the old 1937 name of the Channel Coast Express.

London–Bournemouth–Plymouth: a very old friend reappeared in the shape of the night service on Saturdays and Sundays (10.30 pm from London, arriving Plymouth at 8.33 am), a resumption of the night service first inaugurated by Tourist Motor Coaches in 1930 (see Chapter 4).

Bournemouth–Plymouth: an additional evening journey was introduced between Bournemouth and Exeter.

London–Bristol: the service was increased to 5 journeys per day, one of which continued through from Bristol to Weston-super-Mare and vice versa: this was in addition to the Marlborough–Weston-super-Mare feeder service, which continued to operate.

Portsmouth–Bournemouth–South Coast Express: an extra journey was introduced between Portsmouth and Bournemouth, making 10 journeys daily in that direction only.

London–Penzance: the development of services to and from Cornwall was a particular feature of the post-war build-up and in Summer 1949 the London–Penzance service sprouted yet another branch—the daily feeder service between Exeter, Tavistock, Liskeard, St Austell, Falmouth, and Helston. At the same time, the Exeter–Newquay connection was extended to and from Perranporth. This was all pioneer work, to places previously unserved.

Bournemouth–Ilfracombe: two additional journeys were introduced, Bournemouth–Taunton and return, and Yeovil–Bournemouth and return, providing both earlier and later services on these roads.

New composite timetables were also added—Portsmouth–Plymouth–Penzance and Portsmouth–Taunton–Weston-super-Mare. These composite timetables, besides giving the public useful details of connections, were often operated as 'through duplicates' on busy summer days. The same is true of all the feeder services, which frequently become through coaches (eg London–Exeter–Newquay) on busy days, supplementing the trunk service.

By the summer of 1949 Royal Blue services were back to normal. The demand for coach travel during the post-war years had been greater than anyone could anticipate, doubts as to the future role of express road services had been confounded, and the way now lay open for innovation and expansion. It was time to plan for the future (see Chapter 8).

Meanwhile something must be said of the Winter 1949-50 timetable, which contained one or two important innovations. Perhaps the most significant of these was the continuation of the Bournemouth–Exmouth service throughout the winter months (one journey daily in each direction). The Bournemouth–Plymouth service was also strengthened by the addition of a daily morning journey and a Saturday and Sunday evening journey between Bournemouth and Exeter with corresponding return journeys; one journey in each direction passed through Lyme Regis. The Portsmouth–Plymouth composite timetable was continued from the summer timetable, and for the first time the Royal Blue book gave full details of Associated Motorways services to the South and South-west. These continued in subsequent issues.

During these immediate post-war years, with shortage of vehicles and restricted services, it had been necessary to keep a very strict control on bookings. On some routes agents were required to apply for seat reservations before accepting a booking and four days notice of travel was not uncommon even for midweek bookings. In these days of restrictions, a queue of potential passengers would form at Victoria Coach Station immediately it became known that bookings for Royal Blue summer services were being accepted. So great was the pressure on the limited accommodation available, that the London seat allocation for some peak Saturdays was taken up on the same day that bookings commenced and 'stop-booking' notices were issued.

CHAPTER EIGHT

NEW DEVELOPMENTS 1950-1969

THE year 1950 was marked by two significant developments. The first was the recognition at long last by the Ministry of Transport that English roads could accommodate longer public service vehicles. For many years the 27 ft 6 in overall length restriction had forced body-designers to look upward and had caused the evolution of that essentially British institution, the double-decker. Many European (and other) countries had much more generous length allowances and consequently looked to long single-deckers, sometimes with trailers, for their extra seating capacity. In 1950 a timid first step was made in this country and the permitted overall length was increased to 30 ft, a relaxation of which Royal Blue took immediate advantage. The second factor was the ending of petrol rationing for all vehicles; though hailed at the time with a sigh of relief, few people could foresee that this would usher in a social revolution and alter the behaviour-pattern of almost the entire nation. With an increasing standard of living since then, the private car has gradually become a 'must' for nearly all British families. The consequences have been overcrowded main roads, the spending of millions of pounds on new and improved roads, the swamping of city centres with vehicles, many of them carrying only one person apiece, the use of valuable city-centre sites for car parks, the running down and closure of many local railway lines, and a corresponding depletion and withdrawal of many rural bus services. One wonders whether the authorities, had they possessed the power of foresight, would have been so anxious to give free rein to private transport.

However, as explained in Chapter 9, the impact of private transport on Royal Blue services has so far not proved serious.

NON-STOP JOURNEYS

With the Summer 1950 timetable came the first significant post-war innovation. Non-stop journeys were no new feature, and their importance had been realised in pre-war years (see Chapter 5). But now, in 1950, the importance of rapid transport for the conveyance of holidaymakers wishing to get from home to destination with the least possible delay was recognised as a vital factor in the further expansion of traffic. The following three new non-stop facilities were introduced:

Brighton–Torquay–Totnes: Saturdays and Sundays only in each direction in 11 hours.

London–Ilfracombe: Saturdays and Sundays only in each direction in 10 hours.

London–Weymouth: Saturdays and Sundays and Mondays from London; Fridays, Saturdays and Sundays from Weymouth in 5¾ hours.

These rapid journeys (which of course included refreshment breaks en route) represented savings of 45 min to 1 hour on normal running times and were an instant success. Minor additions in the same timetable included an extra daily journey Bournemouth–Plymouth (not in reverse direction), and an additional Bournemouth–Lyme Regis journey in each direction. Three new composite timetables were added to save both passengers and booking agents delving into two or three separate timetables: these were London–Bournemouth–Axminster, Portsmouth–Bournemouth–Exeter–Cornwall, and Putney–Plymouth. The latter is of particular significance, as it represents an early recognition of the importance of catering for the outer-suburban development of London as distinct from traffic to and from the centre; in later years, this was to lead to important innovations.

The Winter 1950-51 timetable showed little difference from the previous winter, except that the London–Axminster and

Putney–Plymouth composites were perpetuated. An additional London–Southampton journey was introduced in each direction, together with a Sunday evening Salisbury–London service: on the other hand, the daily additional service between Bournemouth–Exeter and return, introduced in the previous winter, was dropped owing to lack of support.

DEVELOPMENT OF NIGHT SERVICES

In 1951 occurred another of those extraneous events that permanently affect the public's travelling habits. Up to this date, night journeys were limited to the 10.30 pm London–Bournemouth 'theatre' facility and the long-standing London–Plymouth (via Bournemouth) journey on Saturdays and Sundays. But the Festival of Britain in 1951 engendered a new demand from people who wished to 'pop up to London for the day to see the show' and come back overnight. The following journeys were accordingly introduced:

(a) 7.0 am Bristol–London on Weds and Sats, non-stop from Marlborough, arriving London 12.0 noon. 11.0 pm London–Bristol on Weds and Sats, non-stop to Marlborough, arriving Bristol 4.0 am.

(b) 7.30 am Weymouth–London on Weds and Sats, non-stop, arriving London 12.53 pm. 10.30 pm London–Weymouth on Weds and Sats, non-stop, arriving Weymouth 3.53 am.

(c) 10.0 pm Ilfracombe–London on Fri nights, arriving London 8.19 am. 10.30 pm London–Ifracombe on Sat nights, arriving Ilfracombe 8.49 am.

(d) 8.0 pm Penzance–London on Fri night, with feeder services at 8.55 pm Newquay–Exeter and 7.35 pm Helston–Exeter; all arriving London 8.21 am.
8.0 pm London–Penzance on Sat nights, with connections at Exeter at 3.37 am for Newquay (arrive 7.26 am) and Helston (arrive 8.46 am); arriving Penzance at 8.21 am.

(e) The old London–Plymouth night journey was revised to operate via Basingstoke and Salisbury (instead of via Bournemouth) and was provided on Fris in addition to Sats and Suns.
A corresponding new night coach was also introduced on Fris and Sats at 10.0 pm Plymouth–London via Salisbury and Basingstoke.

Quite a considerable venture, but one which succeeded beyond expectations; it soon became apparent that, apart from day visitors to the Festival of Britain, the journeys were extensively used by holidaymakers, who found that night travel in modern vehicles was quite tolerable and saved days spent in travelling. From this time onward, the night journey was firmly established as an integral part of the Royal Blue network.

FURTHER DEVELOPMENT

Apart from these night facilities, the Summer 1951 timetable was much the same as Summer 1950, all the non-stop journeys of 1950 being repeated. The extra journey London–Southampton and return, introduced in Winter 1950-51, was also perpetuated.

After so much activity, a little breathing space was obviously required and the Winter 1951-2 timetable was almost an exact replica of the previous winter's. There were minor changes, however: the 10.0 pm London–Bournemouth night coach ran on Sundays in addition to Wednesdays and Saturdays and an 8.15 am Exeter–Bournemouth service was operated on Saturdays and Sundays.

The Bournemouth–Ilfracombe timetable was expanded to show through connections from Portsmouth and Brighton, and a new Putney–Bournemouth–Ilfracombe composite appeared, as further evidence of the growing importance of outer-suburban traffic.

The Summer 1952 timetable consolidated and extended the innovations of the preceding two years. The night coaches introduced the previous summer were all continued, except that the London–Weymouth return was confined to Saturdays (dropping Wednesdays), and the London–Penzance operation and feeder services were stepped up to Fridays and Saturdays in each direction. Generally, the night coaches from London were put back to 11.30 pm and the long-standing London–Bournemouth late journey was also delayed half an hour (11.0 pm instead of 10.30 pm). A further adjustment was that, on Fridays and Saturdays the London–Plymouth night coach operated direct between Exeter and Plymouth, instead of via Torquay, reaching Plymouth in $10\frac{1}{4}$ hours (and similarly in the reverse direction).

The non-stop journeys had proved so successful that they were considerably revised and extended as follows:

> London–Torquay–Brixham: Sats and Suns only in each direction, non-stop London–Torquay in 8¾ hours, with a supplementary journey 3 hours later London–Totnes, non-stop to Torquay.
> London–Minehead–Lynton: Sats and Suns only in each direction, reaching Minehead in 7¾ hours and Lynton in 9¼ hours.
> London–Swanage: Sats and Suns only in each direction in 5¼ hours.
> London–Newquay–Perranporth: Sats and Suns only in each direction, reaching Newquay in 11½ hours.

The previous London–Weymouth non-stop was extended to and from Sidmouth. The London–Bude non-stop was revised to operate between London and Westward Ho!; for the introduction of a daily Taunton–Bude service in place of the Saturday/Sunday only service commenced in 1948, gave a connection with the London–Taunton non-stop, which was still available.

Other important developments in 1952 were the extension of the Dartmouth journeys to and from Kingsbridge and Salcombe, and one Bournemouth–Bridgwater journey in each direction to and from Weston-super-Mare. Extra journeys were introduced at midday and Saturday evenings, London–Bournemouth; midday on Fridays, Saturdays, and Sundays, London–Salisbury, with the evening service Salisbury–London increased to Fridays, Saturdays, and Sundays (instead of Sundays only); and afternoon, Torquay–Salisbury. The Portsmouth–Bournemouth–Weston-super-Mare composite timetable was expanded to Putney and Brighton–Bournemouth–Weston-super-Mare, and a new Putney and Brighton–Bournemouth–Ilfracombe composite was included. Altogether, another major step forward in the development of the Royal Blue network.

Winter 1952-3 brought no significant changes over the previous year, one or two minor deletions being balanced by small additions.

Summer 1953, however, was another period of dramatic development, well illustrating the shrewd management of Royal Blue. This was, of course, Coronation Year, when London became the centre of the world for a season and everyone reckoned on 'Going up to Town to see the decorations and celebrations'. So Royal Blue introduced additional journeys (principally overnight) on specified dates throughout the summer on the following routes to enable passengers to spend a day in London sightseeing:

Plymouth–London and return	Weymouth–London and return
Penzance–London and return	Bristol–London and return
Ilfracombe–London and return	Bournemouth–London (return on the normal late night journey)

Another highly significant innovation was the establishment of the Medway Towns Joint Service with Maidstone & District Motor Services Ltd. It was fully realised by now that if Royal Blue was to retain and expand its traffic, it would be necessary to pay special attention to the increasing populations of the towns adjacent to London. Under modern conditions, people would no longer be content to travel into the centre of London, change coaches and proceed to their destinations in the South-west; direct services were called for and Royal Blue realised that if they were not first in the field others would step in and meet the need. The Medway Towns service was the first practical recognition of this trend. It began at Gillingham and operated via Chatham, Maidstone, Sevenoaks, and Westerham, thence to Portsmouth, Bournemouth, Exeter, Torquay, Paignton, and Totnes. The journeys provided were one in each direction Gillingham–Bournemouth on Mondays to Fridays inclusive, and one in each direction Gillingham–Totnes on Saturdays and Sundays. Two new feeder services into Cornwall were also started during this eventful summer:

(a) Exeter–Crediton–Hatherleigh–Bude–Delabole–Polzeath and return: Saturdays and Sundays only.
(b) Exeter–Moretonhampstead–Dartmoor–Tavistock–Callington–Looe and return: Saturdays and Sundays only.

The Exeter–Helston feeder service was also re-routed via Launceston, Bodmin, and Truro, reducing the running time by 35 min, and its previous route was covered by an additional daily feeder Exeter–Tavistock–Liskeard–St Austell–Truro. Finally, on the Cornwall services, the London–Perranporth non-stop was curtailed at Newquay.

On other routes also, important additions were made in Summer 1953:

London–Plymouth: the night service, ex-Plymouth was augmented by an 8.30 pm departure on Sundays.

London–Weston-super-Mare: a night service was introduced at 11.0 pm from London to Weston on Saturdays; this was a normal 'stopping' service, augmenting the existing 11.0 pm London–Bristol non-stop. A balancing journey was operated at 6.10 pm from Weston to London on Saturdays.

London–Bude: the non-stop journey London–Bude and vice versa was reintroduced on Sats and Suns in addition to the daily Taunton–Bude (with London connections).

London–Ilfracombe: a new non-stop made its appearance, London–Minehead–Porlock Weir (via Blue Anchor) and vice versa on Saturdays; this was in addition to the London–Minehead–Lynton non-stop. The new non-stop reached Minehead in just under 7½ hours. The London–Ilfracombe (and vice versa) night service was also made non-stop between London and Taunton, reducing the journey time by 45 min.

London–Exmouth: additional non-stops were introduced at 8.50 am (Sats and Suns) and 3.0 pm (Fris, Sats, and Suns) London–Weymouth, and 3.30 pm (Fris, Sats, and Suns) Weymouth–London. The London–Sidmouth and return non-stops were extended to Exmouth and the London–Weymouth night service was operated on Fris and Suns in addition to Sats.

Bournemouth–Ilfracombe: one Bournemouth–Yeovil journey in each direction was extended to Crewkerne and Chard.

With the Portsmouth–Bournemouth–Cornwall composite expanded and extended to Brighton, the Royal Blue timetable was now a 56-page book.

Winter 1953-4 services remained the same as the previous winter, with minor alterations and with one important newcomer. The Isle of Wight had not been covered since 1939, when the old coach/air service ceased, but now at last in October 1953 arrangements were concluded with Red Funnel Steamers for through coach/steamer bookings to and from the Island via Southampton–West Cowes. Special connecting timetables were included to the Isle of Wight, utilising existing Royal Blue services (a) From London, (b) From Plymouth, Torquay, Exeter etc, (c) From Brighton and the South Coast. Not so fast as the old coach/air service but a good second best! The through bookings included travel on Southern Vectis buses from West Cowes to various popular centres on the Island.

In 1954 agreement was reached with most of the major express service operators throughout the country for the introduction of a standard express service ticket, 6 in x 4 in; this was a useful step forward in assisting booking agents and operators' staff to deal with the increasing volume of work more expeditiously. This summer saw a further major increase in non-stop journeys, night services, and the exploitation of new traffic potentials, brief details being as follows:

London–Bournemouth: one additional journey daily in each direction, together with a new daily evening non-stop journey Bournemouth–London.

South Coast–Bournemouth–S Devon: a new night service on Fris and Sats, leaving Brighton 10.0 pm, Bournemouth, 3.25 am, thence to Exeter and Totnes, with a corresponding journey leaving Totnes at 9.50 pm (Fris and Sats) for Brighton (7.32 am) with connections to and from Margate.

Medway Towns Service: extended from Totnes to Plymouth on Sats and Suns. In order to tap the traffic potential to the full, a supplementary journey in each direction was also introduced on Sats and Suns between Gillingham and Bournemouth via Maidstone, Tonbridge, and Tunbridge Wells.

London–Bristol–Weston-super-Mare: a new morning non-stop journey on Sats and Suns from London to Bristol. The night service was also rationalised and operated at 11.30 pm London–Bristol on Weds, Fris, and Sats (not non-stop), while the Sat journey at 6.10 pm from Weston to London was retimed to 11.30 pm Bristol–London, to give the first 'up' night service.

London–Ilfracombe: the night service was extended to Fris and Sats in each direction and the London–Westward Ho! non-stop became a daily operation; in addition, the regular daily service between London and Ilfracombe and vice versa was re-routed between Taunton and Ilfracombe via the more direct Bampton–Barnstaple road, leaving the route via Minehead, Exford, and Lynton to be covered by the Bournemouth–Ilfracombe service.

London–Exmouth: the London–Weymouth night service was extended to Exmouth and discontinued on Suns; a new 'up' night service was introduced Exmouth–London on Fris and Sats.

London–Cornwall: new non-stops on Sats and Suns London–Helston and London–Penzance and vice versa. The Exeter–Helston daily feeder service was extended to and from Porthleven, and the Exeter–Truro (via St Austell) feeder was diverted to Mevagissey instead of Truro.

The Isle of Wight facilities, introduced the previous winter, were of course continued during the summer and several new connecting, composite timetables made their appearance; from this time onward, the Associated Motorways timetables were excluded from the Royal Blue book, but a full-page list of all Associated Motorways routes was given.

Generally, the winter services had not developed as rapidly as the summer, but winter 1954-5 was an exception. For the first time, non-stop and night services began to appear throughout the winter months, viz:

Bournemouth–London: 5.0 pm daily, non-stop.
London–Plymouth: night service on Fris and Suns in each direction.
London–Weymouth: non-stop, night service on Sats, with a balancing 7.30 am Weymouth–London.

The night coach from London to Bournemouth was also increased to run nightly throughout the week, the Monday to Tuesday and Thursday to Friday services running via Guildford, Aldershot, and Alton. One Bournemouth–Totnes coach in each direction was extended to Kingsbridge, and one Bournemouth–Portsmouth journey in each direction was diverted via Lymington and Brockenhurst, connecting at the former with boats to and from the Isle of Wight. This was of great assistance to passengers from the West going to or from the Island, as it eliminated the longer journey via Southampton.

But perhaps the boldest innovation was operating the Exeter–Penzance service throughout the winter, linking at Exeter to and from Bournemouth and London. For the first time Cornwall had a daily, all-the-year, express road service and this was a true test of the value of linking facilities. The experiment proved a great success and other Cornish feeder routes subsequently became all-the-year operations. For Christmas 1954, Royal Blue offered the people of Cornwall a special week's holiday in London, with six days full board at a good hotel (including Christmas dinner), a conducted coach tour of London with admission to museums, galleries, etc, and reserved seats for 'Cinderella on Ice', all for £15 19s 0d (£15.95) including coach fare. It was a fine way of making the new winter coach service known to the inhabitants of the far West!

By 1955 Royal Blue had exhausted most of the potential for non-stop and night journeys, though the Summer timetable included one or two minor alterations and additions:

London–Weston-super-Mare: the London–Bristol morning non-stop
   journey was extended to Weston and operated daily instead of Sats
   and Suns only, with a corresponding daily non-stop Bristol–London
   (instead of Weds and Sats only).
London–Swanage: an additional non-stop was introduced in each
   direction on Sats and Suns, making 2 each way at weekends.
London–Cornwall: an additional feeder service was introduced on Sats
   between Exeter–Looe and vice versa in conjunction with the night
   service to and from London.
On the other hand, the London–Lynton non-stop was discontinued
   on Sundays.

But during this year the company concentrated on tapping the
growing population potential to the north-west of London and
early in 1955 an application was submitted for a new High
Wycombe–Salisbury service, linking for points West. It was
granted after a hearing at Winchester on 24 February 1955 and
came into operation with the summer timetable. This new service
was routed via Cookham, Maidenhead, Reading, Newbury, and
Andover, and consisted of a down journey from High Wycombe
on Saturdays, Sundays, and Mondays, and an up journey from
Salisbury on Fridays, Saturdays and Sundays.

Other small additions in Summer 1955 consisted of :

A Sunday 'hospital visitors' coach from Bournemouth to two large hospitals in the Alton area and return.
On the Medway Towns Service, the Gillingham–Bournemouth supplementary journey via Tonbridge was discontinued on Suns, but a similar
   journey was operated on Sats and Suns Gillingham–Portsmouth, and
   similarly in the reverse direction. The Mon to Fri Gillingham–Bournemouth and return were made daily.

The extension of one Bournemouth–Totnes and return
journey to and from Kingsbridge was retained from the previous
winter timetable, as also was the diversion via Brockenhurst and
Lymington (for Isle of Wight).

The national rail strike of June 1955 threw a great deal of
temporary additional traffic on to express road services but its
long-term effects were an undermining of confidence in public
transport, especially when followed two years later by the
national bus strike.

Winter 1955-6 saw no significant developments: the Alton
hospital service continued throughout the winter and the even-

ing journey Bournemouth–Exeter and vice versa on Fridays, Saturdays, and Sundays was extended to Torquay and Totnes. On the other hand, the Marlborough–Weston-super-Mare via Wells feeder service was taken off from November to March inclusive (except for two weeks at Christmas) and the London–Weymouth Saturday night service (and corresponding return journey) introduced the previous winter, was discontinued.

Summer 1956 was marked by two new developments. First, the tapping of outlying centres of population around London was taken a step further by the introduction of a new joint service with Southdown Motor Services between East Grinstead and Totnes via Crawley, Horsham, Petworth, Petersfield, Winchester, Bournemouth, Exeter, and Torquay. This was operated on Saturdays and Sundays only, one journey each way East Grinstead–Bournemouth and a second through journey each way East Grinstead–Totnes (11 hours). Secondly, in view of the rapid growth of car traffic on summer Saturdays, which was already beginning to cause serious traffic jams and delays on the main roads to the South-west, Royal Blue introduced 7.0 am Saturday only non-stop journeys from London to Weymouth, Newquay, Helston, and Penzance during July and August. These were, in effect, advance duplicates to the main non-stop journeys, but by getting away from Victoria Coach Station approximately one hour earlier, they were able to avoid the holiday exodus of private cars. This is just a small example, but it shows the rapid adaptation to new circumstances and the fertile flow of new ideas which characterised Royal Blue management in the post-war years.

Other changes took place in the same summer, principally affecting non-stop journeys, viz :

London–Weymouth: the Saturday non-stop journeys at midnight ex-London and 7.30 am ex-Weymouth were discontinued.
London–Cornwall: the Sat and Sun non-stop journey to and from Helston was extended to Porthleven and Marazion. In addition, new Fri night non-stops were introduced from London at 9.0 pm to Newquay, Helston, and Penzance; again, these were advance reliefs to the main night services, to clear holiday traffic from Victoria Coach Station as quickly as possible.
London–Ilfracombe: the London–Westward Ho! and vice versa non-

Page 125 (top) A Bristol L6B built in 1948, one of the first post-war coaches; *(centre)* R. A. Pryor's preserved ex Royal Blue 'Bristol' in the Porte D'Orléans, Paris, on 14 August 1967. The other vehicle is a Renault TN6; *(below)* Bristol LS6G, as built in 1952, in the 'Valley of Rocks'

Page 126 (*above*) Southern National coach 'on hire' to Royal Blue on the outskirts of London; (*below*) front and rear views of Bristol ECW coach at Square Station, Bournemouth. Later deliveries of 'LS' coaches (as here) dispensed with the front 'quarter lights'

stop was diverted at Barnstaple to Ilfracombe instead, with a connection
at Taunton to and from Westward Ho! during the peak summer
months only.
Medway Towns Service: extra journeys were introduced on Sats only at
8.30 am Gillingham–Plymouth and 7.0 am Plymouth–Gillingham,
non-stop as between Dorking and Dorchester.

Other minor alterations were the extension of the Friday,
Saturday, and Sunday journey London–Salisbury and vice
versa through to Exeter, and the diversion of the Bournemouth–
Chard and vice versa, daily, at Ilminster to Taunton, instead
of Chard.

Opportunity was taken this summer to improve the layout
and grouping of services in the timetable book and also to
include a special page summarising the non-stop journeys
'recommended for Friday Night, Saturday and Sunday Travel'.
The book was now 72 pages.

The services operated during Winter 1956-7 were virtually the
same as the previous year, the only significant change being the
operation of the Bournemouth–Totnes and return journey direct
via Bere Regis to Dorchester, instead of via Wareham and Wool,
cutting 20 min off the running time. The Wareham–Wool
route was covered by the Bournemouth–Exmouth service,
which was also diverted via Abbotsbury and the coast road
between Weymouth and Bridport.

From the end of the War until November 1956 it had been
a story of unqualified success and headlong development for
Royal Blue, but then occurred two events which were to slow
down expansion and lead to some loss of public confidence. First
was the ill-famed 'Suez Crisis', which from November 1956
until the spring of 1957 led to fuel rationing and the temporary
deletion of some services. The unsettled international situation
caused a certain hesitation among the public in making holiday
plans. Secondly came the disastrous fortnight's strike of operating
staff from 20 July 1957 at the peak of the holiday season. There
can be no doubt that these two events caused Royal Blue to
experience its first severe setback since 1946 (see Chapter 9 for
the effect on passenger figures).

The summer service for 1957 was largely a matter of 'trim-

H

ming sails to the prevailing wind'. The Suez affair persisted late into the spring, so Royal Blue deferred the introduction of summer services for two months, to the end of May, with a number of journeys put back until the end of the first week in June. There were also small cuts in services compared with the previous summer, viz :

> London–Bournemouth: the night service ex-London was restricted to Fris, Sats, and Suns, instead of daily, and the midday journey from Bournemouth to London was confined to Sats instead of daily.
> London–Swanage: one of the two non-stops in each direction was restricted to Sats, instead of Sats and Suns.
> London–South Devon: a daily Salisbury–Paignton journey in each direction was discontinued.
> London–North Devon: the morning service from Salisbury to Highbridge each day was deleted.

But it was not all a story of retrenchment and even in adverse circumstances the company was able to introduce one or two useful innovations. Perhaps the most significant was the daily operation of the High Wycombe–Salisbury service during the month of August only. Royal Blue coaches also 'set wheel' on the Isle of Portland for the first time, with the extension of the daily London–Weymouth non-stop to and from Easton. Developments were also taking place on the London–Weston-super-Mare service, with the deviation of one London–Bristol journey in each direction over a new route from Oxford via Lechlade, Cirencester, and Stroud; to cover Swindon, the Marlborough–Weston feeder was extended through to London and return, via Oxford, and Swindon. Other additions that summer were :

> London–Plymouth: a new 9.0 am non-stop on Sats and Suns from each end during July and August, performing the journey in 9¾ hours.
> London–Ilfracombe: a new 7.15 am London–Ilfracombe non-stop on Sats from mid-July to mid-August, with a corresponding 8.0 am Ilfracombe–London.
> London–Bude: a new night non-stop on Fris and Sats from each terminal from mid-July to mid-August.
> Bournemouth–South Devon: the daily Bournemouth–Exeter and return was extended through to Paignton.
> Bournemouth–North Devon: one of the Ilfracombe–Bournemouth journeys was diverted via Lynton and Minehead on Sats and Suns only, retaining the former route via Barnstaple and Bampton on Mons to Fris.

Medway Towns Service: through bookings were inaugurated to and from Gravesend on connecting services operated by Maidstone & District.

The two small route alterations, mentioned under Winter 1956-7, were also continued under the summer services.

The traffic recession following November 1956 was bound to be reflected in the winter timetable, when the passenger potential was at its lowest, and the Winter 1957-8 timetable contained the following cuts, compared with the previous year:

London–Bournemouth:, 1 daily journey in each direction London–Southampton replaced by a Sat only London–Bournemouth and vice versa. The night coach ex-London was also confined to Fris, Sats, and Suns, as during the previous summer.
Bournemouth–Totnes: the evening journey in each direction on Fris, Sats, and Suns was discontinued on Sats.
Bournemouth–North Devon: the morning Bournemouth–Bridgwater and vice versa journey was discontinued from November to March inclusive (except Christmas week).
Bournemouth–Portsmouth: the last journey (8.30 pm) from each terminal was made Sats and Suns only, instead of daily.

Not large cuts, but sufficient to show that the years of expansion were temporarily halted. A first step was made towards a slight speeding up of services—only a matter of minutes but a recognition of the better performance of modern vehicles.

The summer services for 1958 were introduced on the same date as in 1956 (ie end of March) but obviously the company had to tread warily in the light of the previous year's recession and some journeys, including most of the non-stops, were confined to the mid-June to mid-September period, or else were operated on Saturdays and Sundays only before and after that midsummer peak period. Nevertheless, there were some innovations, with an eye to a brighter future:

London–Salcombe: an additional non-stop on Sats and Suns in each direction, during July and August.
London–Cornwall: a new feeder service on Sats and Suns during July and August, Exeter–Launceston–Wadebridge–Padstow–Porth Beach and vice versa. The Fri night London–Penzance non-stop was advanced to 7.15 pm in order to arrive in Penzance in time for the Sat boat to the Scilly Isles, while in the reverse direction a new Sat night Penzance–London non-stop was provided during July and August to connect with the Scilly Isles boat.
London–Mevagissey: a new non-stop on Sats and Suns in each direction, performing the journey in just under 12 hours.

Bournemouth–Portsmouth: a new journey at 5.7 pm on Fris, Sats, and Suns from Southampton (Royal Pier) to Bournemouth for the benefit of boat passengers.

Medway Towns Service: the service became Gillingham–Totnes only (with Plymouth connections) but a new Sunday feeder was operated in each direction between Gillingham and Portsmouth via Tunbridge Wells. More important was the provision of a new through night service on Fris from Gillingham to Newquay, with a corresponding night journey in the other direction on Sats.

There were also one or two deletions compared with the previous summer, the principal one being the reduction of the High Wycombe–Salisbury service to its 1955 level, as the daily operation during August had proved a little too ambitious.

The London–Southampton return journey, daily, was also replaced by a London–Bournemouth journey on Fridays, Saturdays, and Sundays only, similar to the previous winter adjustment, while the midday Saturday journey Bournemouth–London was cancelled. The 8.0 am Ilfracombe–London non-stop on Saturdays only was also discontinued.

So far, the tapping of outlying populations around London had not extended into Essex, but on 4 July 1958 a through-booking arrangement was concluded with Eastern National in respect of their London–Southend-on-Sea service. In subsequent issues of the Royal Blue timetable, details were included of connecting services Southend–London–Bournemouth and the South-west.

Experience of the summer 1958 operations had shown that while there had been a slight revival of traffic compared with 1957, it had by no means approached the old 1956 level and until there was a more buoyant trend, consideration would have to be given to restricting services. With this in view, the Winter 1958-9 timetable was designed to run right through to mid-May 1959; but to cater for such additional traffic as might arise outside the main summer season, the following extra journeys were included, to operate for two weeks in October, three weeks around Christmas, and again from 20 March until the main summer service started:

9.0 am London–Bournemouth non-stop. 11.0 am Plymouth–London 6.20 pm Taunton–Ilfracombe feeder via Minehead and Lynton and

7.10 am in the reverse direction (not over the Christmas period).
11.30 am and 5.0 pm London–Bristol: 11.0 am and 5.30 pm Bristol–
London:
The Exeter–Helston and return feeder service on the Cornwall route.

In addition, there were small cuts in the basic winter timetable: eg the London–Bournemouth night coach ceased
entirely, the last journey in each direction Bournemouth–
Portsmouth was further reduced to Sundays only, and the
Bournemouth–Bridgwater (and vice versa) daily journey was
confined to Fridays, Saturdays, and Sundays, with daily operation during the 'fringe' periods mentioned above.

But on the credit side, new coach/air links were established
to and from Jersey and Guernsey in conjunction with Jersey
Airlines (later British United Airways), utilising existing Royal
Blue journeys. Connections with the air services were provided
at Southampton Airport from the London direction; Hurn
Airport from Taunton, Yeovil, North Devon, etc; and Exeter
Airport from Plymouth, Paignton, etc.

The summer services for 1959 came into operation on 15 May
and included the new Eastern National links (Southend–
London–Bournemouth) and full details of the Jersey/Guernsey
coach/air services, initiated the previous winter. There were
also two new non-stops, London–Mevagissey on Saturdays and
Sundays, and Looe–London on Saturdays, together with a new
3.20 am coach from Bournemouth to London on Sundays via
Aldershot and Guildford, connecting with the Saturday night
service from the West. But apart from these limited innovations,
the Company was still proceeding warily and the opportunity
was taken to 'trim down' journeys, particularly non-stops, as
follows:

London–Exmouth non-stop deleted on Mons but continued on Sats
and Suns.
Exmouth–London non-stop deleted on Suns but continued on Fris and
Sats.
London–Easton and vice versa non-stop deleted on Tues, Weds, and
Thurs but continued on other days of the week.
The second London–Swanage non-stop deleted on Suns but continued
on Sats.
Weymouth–London non-stop deleted on Fris but continued on Sats
and Suns.

London–Brixham non-stop deleted on Suns but continued on Sats.
Porthleven–London non-stop deleted on Suns but continued on Sats.
London–Looe non-stop deleted on Suns but continued on Sats.
Porlock Weir–London and vice versa non-stop truncated at Porlock.

In addition, one journey per day was taken out of the Bournemouth–Portsmouth service in each direction; the Exeter–Porth Beach and return feeder service was reduced to Saturdays only; the London–Bristol night service was deleted on Wednesdays; and one journey in each direction between London and Salisbury was operated on Fridays to Mondays instead of daily.

The Winter 1959-60 service was exactly the same as the previous winter, apart from adjustment to timings and the shortening of the spring 'fringe' period, which was to start on 11 April, instead of 20 March. By the spring of 1960 Royal Blue had stabilised the position arising from the 1957 setback, and from the foregoing it will be seen that trimming services is probably as difficult as expanding them.

There is not a great deal to record for Summer 1960: the summer services did not start until 1 June (two weeks later than the previous year) but otherwise operations were more or less stabilised at the 1959 level. It is worth recording that a new non-stop was introduced on Saturdays in each direction between Kingston and Weymouth to cater for outer-London traffic, and a new section of route was opened up on Saturdays and Sundays by a connecting journey in each direction, Yeovil–Somerton–Bridgwater–Williton–Minehead–Lynton–Ilfracombe. An additional 8.50 am non-stop was introduced from London to Ilfracombe on Saturdays and Sundays and the London–Looe Saturday non-stop was diverted via Seaton (Cornwall) Holiday Camp in each direction. New journeys also appeared on Saturdays between Bournemouth and Brighton and vice versa, non-stop as between Bournemouth and Portsmouth but, on the other hand, a daily afternoon journey Bournemouth–Portsmouth and vice versa was discontinued. Also discontinued were the 3.20 am (Sundays) Bournemouth–London night journey, introduced the previous summer, and an evening journey Bournemouth–

London except on Saturdays. In a further effort to build up traffic on linking services, new timetables were included showing connecting services between Cornwall, the Midlands, South Wales, the North and Scotland; and also connecting facilities with through bookings between the West and Kent, Sussex, and Essex.

The Winter 1960-61 timetable was the same as the previous winter, except for the addition of an afternoon journey from Exeter to Plymouth direct, during the special periods (ie October, Christmas, and spring); the corresponding 7.0 am Plymouth–Exeter journey was operated on behalf of Associated Motorways to connect with the Cheltenham service. The 2.10 pm Sunday journey from Totnes to Bournemouth was also extended back to Plymouth. During 1960-61 Royal Blue was in effect resting quietly, while traffic revived, before embarking upon the latest series of developments.

By 1961 it was felt that the position had sufficiently recovered to justify some judicious experimentation. The Royal Blue management had always been characterised by the ability to anticipate new traffic demands and in summer 1961 attention was turned to the rapidly expanding air traffic at London (Heath Row) Airport. To cater for people travelling to and from the airport for holidays abroad, three special coach journeys were scheduled to London Airport on Friday evenings from Bournemouth, Exeter, and Bristol, returning from London Airport on Sunday mornings to the same destinations. Again in connection with growing air traffic, daily duplicate coaches were added to the 10.55 am Bournemouth–London and the 12.10 pm London–Bournemouth journeys, calling at Hurn Airport for Channel Islands flights. Some of the services cancelled over the previous few years were also put back : eg one of the London–Newquay non-stops in each direction was extended to Perranporth once more, and two extra non-stops appeared on Saturdays in each direction and one on Sundays on the Bournemouth–Portsmouth–South Coast route. More significant still was the resumption of daily operation on the High Wycombe–Paignton service from mid-June to mid-August.

During the early and late parts of the season (end of April to end of May and mid-September to mid-October) Royal Blue also offered special 8-day holidays in Torquay, Ilfracombe, and Bournemouth to retired people at cheap rates. These holidays included coach fares to the resort, transfer to hotels, full accommodation at the hotel for one week and three local coach tours. A specimen price from London was 10 guineas for the Torquay holiday.

The Winter 1961-2 timetable was marked by similar small improvements : eg the special Christmas period of operation was extended from two to three weeks; the second up journey from South Devon to London was operated on Saturdays throughout the winter in addition to daily during the special periods; the Bournemouth–Bridgwater and vice versa journeys were similarly operated on Fridays and Saturdays throughout the winter; and the Saturdays only Bournemouth–London and return journey was increased to Fridays, Saturdays, and Sundays. But the most significant new development this winter was the operation of the Exeter–Newquay and return feeder service daily during the three special periods (ie October, Christmas, and April)—a further step in the expansion of services into Cornwall, and a pilot-scheme to ascertain whether operation throughout the winter could be justified.

On 24 October 1961 one of the masterpieces of modern engineering was completed—the Tamar Suspension Bridge, connecting Plymouth and Saltash by road, a modern counterpart of Brunel's famous railway bridge, which stands only a few hundred yards down river.

This opened up entirely new patterns of travel for the Plymouth area and that city, previously at a virtual dead-end as far as through road traffic was concerned and connected with Cornwall only by the Saltash passenger ferry and the Torpoint car ferry of very limited capacity, became overnight an important point on a second trunk route from the east into Cornwall. Western National was quick to seize the opportunities offered and local bus services from Looe, Callington, and Forder, previously terminating at Saltash, were immediately extended across the new bridge to Plymouth. Royal Blue was not far behind and in the Summer timetable for 1962 one daily Bourne-mouth–Plymouth journey in each direction was extended across the Tamar Bridge to Bodmin, Truro, and Penzance, giving a second regular daily service in summer to and from Cornwall. Another innovation for this summer was the establishment of Royal Blue/Aer Lingus links, with through bookings London–Bristol–Dublin/Cork, a further extension of coach/air facilities. There were other signs of a healthy revival of traffic; a new daily non-stop London–Bournemouth and vice versa, calling at Hurn Airport; a new Southampton–London non-stop on Saturdays; the Perranporth–London non-stop was operated on Fridays as well as Saturdays and Sundays; and two new Saturday non-stops commenced in each direction on the Bournemouth–Portsmouth–South Coast route.

The services for Winter 1962-3 also included several important new developments. Perhaps most significant was the daily operation throughout the winter of the Exeter–Camelford–Newquay–Perranporth (and vice versa) feeder service, continu-ing the gradual build-up of winter facilities to and from Cornwall. The raising of the speed limit from 30 to 40 mph was also reflected in the 1962-3 timetable where, after a good deal of hard bargaining with staff, the running times of all journeys were speeded up by amounts ranging from 5 to 35 min, according to route.

In recognition of the rapidly-expanding population of Swindon as a satellite town, two daily feeder journeys were provided between Swindon and Marlborough, connecting with the main London–Bristol service. The Bournemouth–London and return journey, operated on Fridays, Saturdays, and Sun-days, the previous winter, was increased to a daily service, and an additional evening non-stop journey was introduced on Fridays and Sundays between London and Bournemouth.

During this winter, Royal Blue also offered special 1-week Bargain Holidays (October to May) at Torquay and Paignton at the very moderate prices of 7 guineas and 6 guineas respectively, plus coach fare.

Also in 1962 the Transport Act divided the British Transport
Commission into separate units, the bus and coach interests
going to the Transport Holding Co, including the entire share
capitals of the Tilling Group of companies. The companies were
enjoined by the Act to operate as separate entities and to declare
dividends arrived at before making any interest charges. This
was an important enactment; in effect it said, 'Although you
are state-owned concerns, you must continue to function as
separate commercial undertakings and show reasonable profits'.

The various experimental services operated in conjunction
with rail closures from 1963 onward are dealt with fully in
Chapter 9.

For the summer of 1963, the speeding-up process of the
previous winter was carried through to the summer schedules,
some of the long-distance Saturday non-stops having as much
as an hour taken off the running time. In the event this proved a
little too optimistic, having regard to general traffic conditions
in the South-west in the summer and some extra running time
has had to be restored subsequently. There were several other
signs of expansion during this summer:

1. A new experimental coastal service of 1 journey per day in each
direction was inaugurated from Minehead via Lynton, Ilfracombe,
Barnstaple, Bideford, Bude, Newquay, Truro, and Falmouth to Helston
and Porthleven.

2. To cater for the large new holiday camp opened by Butlins at Minehead, a through Sat coach was operated in each direction from Plymouth via Exeter to Minehead, duplicating existing stage and express
service timings.

3. The High Wycombe–Salisbury service was operated daily throughout
the period of the summer timetable (26 May to 19 October); after its
hesitant start in 1955, this service had fully justified itself and became
a daily feature during the summer.

4. An additional Sat journey was introduced between Exeter and
Salcombe and vice versa, connecting on and off the night services from
London and the South Coast.

5. A second Sat non-stop was introduced between London–Exmouth
and vice versa, the Sat non-stop London–Westward Ho! and vice versa
was introduced, and a new daily non-stop service of 4¼ hours was
started—11.30 am London–Bristol and 12.0 noon Bristol–London.

6. There were other small additions, which indicated that traffic was
once more showing a buoyant trend: eg the Fri, Sat, Sun, and Mon
journeys London–Bournemouth and London–Salisbury (and vice
versa) were operated daily, the London–Easton non-stop became a
daily operation as London–Weymouth, and the second daily Bourne-

mouth–Kingsbridge and vice versa service was extended down to Salcombe. On the other hand, the Aer Lingus arrangement had not proved successful and was cancelled.

The 1963-4 winter services also included important new features, principally in Cornwall. The Exeter–Helston feeder service became a daily operation throughout the winter and the Perranporth feeder, begun the previous winter, was altered to Plymouth–Launceston–Newquay–Perranporth, connecting at Launceston with the other Cornish services. By this means day return facilities were provided from all principal towns in Cornwall to Plymouth. Another significant alteration was the start of the High Wycombe–Salisbury service (with connections to and from the West) in mid-March 1964, two months before the introduction of the main summer timetable. On the London–Weston-super-Mare service, the Swindon–Marlborough connections ceased, but to serve Swindon adequately, the Marlborough–Weston feeder journeys were extended to and from London via Swindon and Oxford. A new daily non-stop appeared in each direction on the Bournemouth–Portsmouth–South Coast route and the two Bournemouth–Bridgwater journeys, together with the Yeovil–Ilfracombe connecting service via Somerton, Bridgwater, Minehead, and Lynton, were operated daily throughout the winter instead of during the three special periods only (October, Christmas and spring). Salcombe also received a daily winter service for the first time, by the extension of the Bournemouth–Totnes journey in each direction. On the other hand, the Sunday service between Bournemouth and the Alton Hospitals was withdrawn both summer and winter.

The summer of 1964 was marked by further important innovations. In order to perpetuate the previous winter's service between Cornwall and Plymouth, a new Plymouth–Launceston–Bude service was brought into operation. This consisted of one journey daily in each direction and besides acting as a cross-link to several east-west express services, it also replaced the previous Plymouth–Bude through Western/Southern National stage service, which had been broken at Launceston to a connecting facility only.

The High Wycombe service was also extended from Salisbury to serve a new route via Mere, Wincanton, Ilchester, and Honiton to Exeter. Ever on the lookout for new business Royal Blue extended one journey in each direction on the London–Bournemouth service to and from Rockley Sands Holiday Estate at Poole on Saturdays. A new feeder journey was also started on Saturdays to and from the night services at Exeter, via Paignton, Brixham, and Dartmouth to Kingsbridge. Other signs of expansion were a new daily non-stop in each direction London–Bournemouth, the daily operation of the Exeter–Looe (via Moretonhampstead and Callington) feeder service instead of Fridays, Saturdays, Sundays, and Mondays only, and the extension of the daily London–Bristol non-stop in each direction to Weston-super-Mare. On the other side of the picture, the Weymouth–Easton section was discontinued.

During the years of post-war expansion, Exeter had become increasingly important as a focal point for routes fanning out westward into Devon and Cornwall and eastward to London and the South Coast. For interchange purposes, services were so designed to converge on Exeter three times daily and again at night (weekends only) during the summer and twice daily in the winter. On a peak summer day no less than 400 coaches arrive and depart from this centre. For some years the old pre-war coach park in Paul Street, Exeter, had been exhibiting chronic signs of overcrowding, with coaches queuing up to enter but in July 1964 this was remedied by the opening of the fine new bus and coach station in Paris Street. This includes booking-offices, restaurant, waiting-rooms, and every possible facility for travellers, besides ample space for vehicles even on the busiest Saturday. It has contributed greatly to the efficient operation of long-distance coach services.

Another innovation appeared in the Winter 1964-5 timetable —the use of the 24-hour clock in British bus and coach time-tables generally. Once the public had become accustomed to the idea, this system made for greater clarity in timetables, especially in the case of long-distance services and night services, where 'am' and 'pm' had become rather complicated. The Bournemouth–Plymouth route was further developed during this winter, with the journey previously confined to weekends and special periods operating daily and a further Bournemouth–Plymouth and return introduced during the three special periods (October, Christmas, and spring). Otherwise the winter timetable was essentially the same as the previous year. Royal Blue now had a programme of 8-day 'Thrift Holidays' in spring and autumn, with local tours, at Bournemouth, Ilfracombe, and Torquay, and 'Bargain Holidays' at seven different resorts for as little as £5 15s od plus coach fare, for seven nights at the chosen centre.

Mr C. H. Preece, who for 35 years had piloted the affairs of Royal Blue, retired in March 1965, and Mr L. T. Duncan, then appointed traffic manager of Western & Southern National, took over his work. Mr Preece left the company full of vigour, with mind still as active as ever. Although approaching his seventieth year at the time of writing, he is still immersed in many local activities and is a member of the Transport Users Consultative Committee for the South West. Before he retired, Mr Preece planned, negotiated, and saw through the traffic courts yet another important Royal Blue route, serving the outer population belt north of London. This was the Hitchin–Luton–Chesham–Beaconsfield–Windsor–Hartley Wintney–Salisbury service of one journey daily in each direction, which started operation with the 1965 Summer timetable. In the same timetable the Plymouth–Bude cross-linking service was further extended at each end—eastward to Torquay and westward via Tintagel and Delabole to Polzeath. The map was nearing completion in its present form. Summer 1965 was marked by other important changes on the existing services, viz :

London–Bournemouth: a new Basingstoke–London and return daily service and the resumption of the 3.20 am Bournemouth–London (via Guildford) connection with the night services on Sundays, discontinued in 1960. As against this, one London–Bournemouth and return daily non-stop was deleted.

London–Exmouth: a new daily journey in each direction Bournemouth–Seaton (Devon) and the extension of the 7.40 am London–Weymouth non-stop (Saturdays) to Exmouth.

London–South Devon: a new daily journey Salisbury–Brixham and return, plus the daily operation of the 1.10 pm London–Plymouth and 8.30 am Exeter–London, instead of weekends only.

London–Cornwall: extension of the Exeter–Perranporth day feeder service to and from St Agnes and Portreath, with the Exeter–Polzeath feeder confined to Sats only in view of the new Torquay–Polzeath service.

London–Weston-super-Mare: an additional non-stop journey in each direction on Fris and Sats London–Bristol, plus the down night service operating additionally on Wed nights and the up night service on Sat nights.

Medway Towns Service: the Sunday feeder Gillingham–Portsmouth via Tunbridge Wells and return was deleted.

The Royal Blue timetable book now ran to 104 pages.

Winter 1965-6 saw the loss of yet another old and tried 'servant' of Royal Blue, for it was then that, in the cause of rationalisation, the company handed over their interest in the London–Bristol–Weston-super-Mare 'Greyhound/Royal Blue' service to the Bristol Omnibus Co. But change is the one unchanging factor in all human affairs, and Royal Blue had other items to look to during that winter. The Luton–Salisbury section of the new Hitchin service was resumed from 1 April 1966—Saturdays, Sundays, and Mondays, down, Fridays, Saturdays, and Sundays, up; the new facility proved very successful. On the other hand the High Wycombe service was not recommenced in mid-March this year and awaited the introduction of the full Summer timetable. It was a see-saw winter, with some positive things and some negative: a second daily down journey was started from London to Plymouth at 12.0 noon to balance the up journey operated daily since 1961, but the Yeovil–Ilfracombe connection via Somerton, Bridgwater, and Minehead was cut back to the Christmas and spring periods. The Bournemouth–South Devon service was tidied up, to give three daily journeys in each direction to and from Plymouth, Salcombe and Totnes respectively. On the London–Bournemouth service, a new daily journey was introduced in each direction between Basingstoke and London, together with an evening non-stop London–Bournemouth on Fridays and Saturdays; on the other hand, the two daily Bournemouth–Bridgwater journeys were curtailed at Taunton and one was confined to Fridays, Saturdays, and Sundays only.

By 1966 the traffic build-up since 1957 had levelled off at

about the 1,500,000 passengers per annum mark. It was, there-fore, decided to husband resources and a careful analysis of all journeys was carried out with a view to deleting those inade-quately used, and producing timetables that supplied a basic all-the-year service supplemented by additional journeys in summer.

It was also recognised that all fully loaded duplicates in summer were, in effect, non-stop journeys and a great many of the timetabled non-stops were accordingly removed from the timetable, except where they provided services not covered by regular scheduled journeys. The main object of this policy was to use vehicles more efficiently by not committing them to fixed timetabled journeys which might at certain times prove unwanted. In addition, the passenger statistics had shown a falling-off in London traffic, compensated by a growth of provincial cross-country traffic; it was, therefore, all the more important to thin down any unwarranted timings to and from London, so that vehicles could be available for duplication else-where. Before outlining the considerable changes brought about in the Summer 1966 timetable, note must be made of yet another new facility. For many years, a summary of connecting journeys between Essex and the South-west had appeared in each timetable issue, but in 1966 a through joint service was established with Eastern National between Southend/Sudbury–Brentwood–Salisbury–Exeter–Torquay–Brixham, down on Fri-day nights, returning on Saturday nights. What, then, was the shape of the new 1966 timetable?

London–Bournemouth: the service was completely revised to give 12 journeys per day (2 non-stop), with an additional non-stop in each direction on Fris and Sats, plus the established night coaches. Times were rearranged to give an approximately hourly service leaving both London and Bournemouth on the hour. The London Airport specials were discontinued in view of the poor loadings achieved.

London–Exmouth: the basic timetable was not disturbed but all non-stops, with the exception of the London–Weymouth and return daily non-stop, were restricted to Sats only, as was also the Bournemouth–Swanage feeder service (previously Sats and Suns); the 9.15 am London–Exmouth Saturday non-stop ceased altogether.

London–South Devon: the only alterations to the basic service were the curtailment of the daily Salisbury–Brixham and return at Paignton and the truncation of the Saturday feeder to and from the night service at Brixham (instead of Kingsbridge). The non-stops were com-

pletely revised and only the following were retained on Saturdays
only:
  8.15 am London–Brixham and 9.15 am Brixham–London.
  10.15 am London–Salcombe and 10.30 am Salcombe–London.
London–Cornwall: a new daily feeder service was introduced between
  Exeter and Bude. Although this is mentioned in Chapter 9 under rail
  closures, it is repeated here, as the facility has now become integrated
  into the revised pattern of services and is not a temporary experiment.
  The Exeter–Porthleven feeder was cut back to Helston but apart from
  this the basic service remained unchanged. The non-stops were drastic-
  ally overhauled and became as follows:

  Sats: 7.30 am London–Perranporth and 9.15 am Perranporth–
    London.
    7.30 am London–Bude–Polzeath and 9.10 am Polzeath–Bude–Lon-
    don.
    7.30 am London–Porthleven and 9.0 am Porthleven–London.
    7.30 am London–Penzance and 8.30 am Penzance–London.
  Night Non-Stop Services: 7.30 (Fris) London–Penzance and 8.35 pm
    (Sats) Penzance–London.
    9.0 pm (Fris) London–Newquay and 9.15 pm (Sats) Newquay–Lon-
    don.
London–Mevagissey: the London–Mevagissey and return non-stop be-
  came Sats only (instead of Sats and Suns); otherwise no change.
London–North Devon: the whole of the Bude services were discontinued,
  being replaced by the new route via Exeter, as mentioned under
  London–Cornwall. The revised service became:
    London–Ilfracombe, 1 journey daily each way, non-stop between
    London and Yeovil.
    1 Sat non-stop each way (via Lynton).
    Night service on Fris and Sats in each direction.
    London–Porlock, 1 Sat non-stop each way.
    Yeovil–Ilfracombe, 1 daily connecting journey each way via Bridg-
    water and Minehead.
    Yeovil–Westward Ho!, 1 daily connecting journey each way via
    Taunton and Barnstaple.
Bournemouth–South Devon: the only alteration was the deletion of the
  long-standing diversion round Bovington Camp, Dorset.
Bournemouth–North Devon: no change but an additional night non-stop
  was introduced at 3.20 am (Sats and Suns) Bournemouth–Westward
  Ho! and 9.20 pm (Fris and Sats) Westward Ho!–Bournemouth.
Bournemouth–Portsmouth: 2 Saturday non-stops in each direction were
  discontinued.
Torquay–Polzeath: cut back to Plymouth–Delabole via Launceston and
  omitting Bude.
Minehead–Ilfracombe–Cornwall: extended to and from Taunton but
  curtailed at Helston.
Medway Towns Service: additional Saturday journeys in each direction,
  Dartford–Bournemouth and Gravesend–Bournemouth.
East Grinstead–Totnes: confined to Sats only, instead of Sats and Suns.

As the summer services were about to begin and after the
timetable books had been issued, news came that the traffic

Page 143 (*above*) No 2213 built in 1957 was one of the first batch of coaches built for Royal Blue since the late 1920s without the roof luggage container; (*below*) Bristol MW6G as new at the 1958 Paignton Coach Rally, in the revised livery introduced with this batch of coaches

Page 144 (above) The first MW6G to be delivered to Royal Blue with the new style body. No 2270 crossing the Tamar Bridge; *(below)* Bristol RELH6G No 2364 leaving the coach station at Exeter

commissioners had granted an important new facility. For some time there had been an encouraging build-up of traffic on the London–Plymouth night service (operated at weekends only) and the bold experiment of operating this throughout the week in each direction was initiated for the summer period. This meant that, for the first time in the history of Royal Blue, a coach was in service somewhere for 24 hours of every day for 5 months of the year.

These then are the summer services which, with slight modification, have continued to 1969. The running times on Saturday non-stop journeys are of academic interest only, in view of the traffic conditions which have been allowed to develop on main roads to and from the West on peak summer Saturdays.

Having standardised the summer operations, the company turned its attention to one or two important new developments in the winter 1966-7 services. In the main, timetables were the same as the previous winter, except that the London–Bournemouth times were rearranged on the hour from each end and the London–Basingstoke and return journey, introduced in 1965, was discontinued. The London–Plymouth night service had proved a success and to test the response during the winter months, arrangements were made for continuous operation during the two-week Christmas period and again from 19 March 1967, adding a further two months to all-the-week night operation. Services into Cornwall also took another step forward by the introduction of new daily feeder services Exeter–Newquay and Exeter–St Austell (via Callington and Liskeard), Helston being covered by a diversion of the Plymouth–Perranporth service from Launceston. The Cornwall feeder services thus became Exeter–Penzance, Exeter–Newquay, Exeter–St Austell, the first two connecting at Launceston for Falmouth and Helston.

The picture was now complete and all important towns in Cornwall were served by daily express services throughout the year. The Hitchin–Salisbury service was also operated for the two-week Christmas period and again from mid-March 1967, as a further experiment in extending the dates of operation of services. From this winter, Royal Blue services were allocated

I

route numbers preceded by an X: eg X1 London–Bournemouth, X3 London–Plymouth.

At the end of the winter (from 19 March to 20 May) the additional daily journey from Ilfracombe to Taunton and vice versa, mentioned in Chapter 9 under rail closures, was introduced; this has now been extended to and from Yeovil and integrated as a permanent feature of the Royal Blue network, being operated daily throughout the winter.

The process of building up cross-London services was continued during summer 1967, when a new Royal Blue/Eastern National/Eastern Counties/Grey Green Joint service came into operation between Ipswich/Southend–Ilfracombe. This consisted of a day-time journey on Saturdays from both Ipswich and Southend, with corresponding journeys from Ilfracombe and together with the Southend/Sudbury–Brixham night services introduced the previous summer, effectively linked the main towns of Essex, plus Ipswich, with the West Country. The other major change of this summer was the deletion of the Taunton–Minehead coastal service to Helston, which had been showing a very poor traffic return. However, the service was replaced by two additional journeys which effectively linked most of the towns on the line of route with the main east-west coach network, viz:

1. A daily additional timing Taunton–Ilfracombe and return via Minehead and Simonsbath (not Lynton).
2. A daily additional facility Helston–Newquay–Camelford–Bude–Exeter and vice versa.

The only section of route left unserved was Bideford–Hartland–Bude.

Another important item was the addition of Bude to the night-service network by the provision of Saturday feeder journeys Exeter–Bude and vice versa.

Other additions this summer were

London–Bournemouth: a new 1.0 am journey on Sats for passengers going to London to join continental tours. One additional journey daily in each direction took in New Milton.
London–South Devon: a new daily 9.30 am London–Exeter non-stop, with a corresponding up journey at 12.50 pm from Exeter. The regular

London–Plymouth night service was now firmly established for the summer months (from the end of March to the beginning of October). London–North Devon: the London–Lynton non-stop, discontinued the previous summer, was resumed on Sats and a Westward Ho!–London non-stop also re-appeared on Sats.
On the Bournemouth–Portsmouth–South Coast route, the Brighton–Totnes (and vice versa) Saturday non-stop became a daily operation.

Another innovation in the Summer 1967 timetable was the inclusion of a very clear, folding, route map, a copy of which appears at the back of this book.

Further changes, mainly by way of developments, were included in the Winter 1967-8 timetable. Firstly must be recorded the deletion of a long-established facility, the Bournemouth–Park Prewett Hospital service; the hospital was covered henceforth by a 'Wilts & Dorset' local bus connection to and from Basingstoke. In its place, however, there commenced an entirely new hospital service on Wednesdays and Sundays throughout the year from Christchurch via Bournemouth, Wareham, and Weymouth to Herrison Hospital north of Dorchester. This change was brought about by the fact that all Hampshire area patients were henceforth being sent to Herrison Hospital, instead of Park Prewett. The 9.0 am London–Bournemouth journey, previously restricted to the Christmas and spring periods, became daily throughout the winter and the Exeter–Newquay feeder service was extended to Perranporth during the Christmas and spring periods. The Bournemouth–Plymouth journey was diverted via Wareham and Weymouth to Dorchester, but Salcombe lost its winter service by curtailment at Kingsbridge. Finally, a Bournemouth–Taunton journey in each direction was diverted from Yeovil via Chard and Ilminster to Taunton.

In the Summer 1968 timetable, Royal Blue inaugurated no less than four schemes affecting the outer-London and cross-London traffic:

1. A new service was introduced of one journey daily in each direction, London–Guildford–Aldershot–Winchester–Salisbury–Yeovil–Exeter–Plymouth, linking important towns to the South-east of London direct

with South Devon and by connection at Yeovil and Exeter to North Devon and Cornwall. This facility replaced the Saturday only journeys Kingston–Paignton and vice versa and has proved a great success in creating new traffic to the South-west.

2. A new joint service was designed, approved by the traffic commissioners, and brought into operation, of one journey daily in each direction, Stevenage–Hitchin–Luton–St Albans–Basingstoke–Winchester–Southampton–Bournemouth–Weymouth, after the United Counties Omnibus Co Ltd agreed to withdraw their Luton–Bournemouth service.

3. A new facility was introduced, jointly with Eastern Counties Omnibus Co, from Norwich via Newmarket, London, Basingstoke, and Southampton to Bournemouth. This represented the through operation of one existing journey daily in each direction Bournemouth–London and London–Norwich.

4. To tidy up services from the outer areas of north and north-west London, the existing Hitchin and High Wycombe services were combined into a Hitchin–Luton–Chesham–Beaconsfield–Maidenhead–Reading–Newbury–Andover–Salisbury–Mere–Wincanton–Honiton–Exeter route; one journey in each direction, with local bus connections at Maidenhead to and from High Wycombe, plus a direct Sat journey in each direction High Wycombe–Totnes.

Besides these major schemes, there were other lesser developments, viz:

London–Bournemouth: a new 5.0 pm journey on Fris, Sats, and Suns via Ferndown.

Bournemouth–North Devon: Bournemouth–Weston-super-Mare journeys were diverted via Burnham-on-Sea.

Southend/Ipswich–Ilfracombe: operated on Suns in addition to Sats.

Medway Towns Service: Maidstone–Bournemouth Sat journeys extended to and from Sheerness, also Dartford and Gravesend Sat journeys combined into a Gravesend–Dartford–Bournemouth service.

Plymouth–Minehead (Butlins Camp): a second through service in each direction on Sats.

On the other side of the picture, the East Grinstead–Totnes through operation was discontinued, being covered by connecting facilities at Bournemouth between Royal Blue and Southdown Motor Services. The process of weeding out Saturday non-stop journeys was also continued, the following 5 being deleted: Kingston–Weymouth and return, London–Lynton and return, and Bognor–Bournemouth.

The winter 1968-9 services showed another step forward, in that they included several additions and no deletions compared with the previous winter. Most important of the additions was the daily operation throughout the winter of the Exeter–Bude and return feeder service. As mentioned under winter 1966-7, the Ilfracombe–Taunton and vice versa journey was extended to and from Yeovil daily with connection to London.

The London–Guildford–South Devon journey proved so popular during the summer months, that it was reintroduced daily from 30 March 1969, ie some six weeks before the full summer timetable; and the Brighton–Totnes and vice versa daily non-stop journeys were also commenced from 30 March 1969. The Hitchin–Salisbury service continued via Reading, as during the summer, and was operated over the Christmas and spring periods, as the previous winter. Finally, as an experiment, the new Hitchin–Weymouth service was operated daily for ten days over the Easter holiday period.

A further change of ownership took place on 1 January 1969 when, as a result of the Transport Act 1968, the securities of the Western & Southern National Omnibus Companies were transferred to the National Bus Company.

The Summer 1969 timetable continued the pattern of innovation and adaptation which had characterised Royal Blue since its inception, the principal changes compared with Summer 1968 being

1. A special Sat morning journey from London direct to Southampton Airport Reception Office for air connections, returning to London in the afternoon.
2. A new direct service on Sats from London to Pontin's Holiday Camp, Osmington (near Weymouth) and return.
3. The South Coast timetable was revised to include a new direct service daily between Bournemouth and Ramsgate via Brighton and Canterbury, reducing the overall journey time by 1¾ hours.
4. The High Wycombe–Totnes facility was increased from Sats only to Sats and Suns ex High Wycombe and Fris and Sats ex Totnes.

The future is always misty but is now less predictable than ever; over all hangs the new Transport Act with its possible reshaping of public transport facilities generally and in particular its restrictions on drivers' hours of work, which could have widespread repercussions on road transport, already suffering from a chronic shortage of staff. But whatever comes to pass, the Royal Blue network is now an established and essential part of the transport pattern of southern England and one may confidently expect to see the familiar coaches on the West-country roads for years to come.

What lessons can be gleaned from the foregoing pages? First, it must be recalled that every change, every new development, required careful investigation, wise planning, negotiation with other interested parties (including the railways), presentation and argument in the traffic courts, and all the intricate details of final implementation. The amount of work involved in building-up the Royal Blue network has been prodigious and one can only admire the devoted service of staff, from management down through inspectors to drivers, which has created a tradition and a legend unequalled in the coaching world. The constant altera- tions, the unceasing search for new features, the foreseeing of events and trends, so amply brought out in the detail of this and previous chapters, is only another example that where there is life there must be unceasing movement and adaptation. Finally, it is hoped that the preceding chapters will show that the con- cepts of co-ordination, rationalisation and co-operation are not brand new ideas hatched from the 'new professionalism' but have been innate in the transport industry from its infancy. There is nothing new under the sun, yet all things must change marvellously.

CHAPTER NINE

POST-WAR IN GENERAL

A FRIGHTENING WINTER 1962-3

'THE winters now are not what they were when I was a boy—why, I can remember when we used to skate on the pond every year and . . .' The Clerk of the Weather must have heard this sentiment voiced a million times, and, as the winter of 1962-3 got under way, decided to demonstrate that not only could English winters be every bit as severe as 'When I was a boy' but that this particular one would outdo all records for some two centuries! After some preliminary experiments with snow showers and gales at the end of November, all was calm over Christmas Day; but just as people were returning home from holiday, conditions began to deteriorate. Few people suspected, when five Royal Blue services had to be cancelled or curtailed on Boxing Day due to icy roads in the Southampton Area, that this was to be the prelude to a series of stories such as Royal Blue had never before experienced. The next day, the Minehead–Lynton section of the Bournemouth–Ilfracombe service was impassable and on Friday, 28 December, no less than nineteen journeys were cancelled or failed to reach their destination due to ice-bound roads. Then on Saturday, 29 December, a blizzard of unprecedented ferocity hit south-west England and within hours there were snowdrifts 15-20 ft deep in exposed places. All passenger transport in the western counties was brought to a standstill and the Western/Southern National traffic report for 30 December makes gloomy reading indeed—east of a line from Fowey to Newquay, not a wheel turned apart from Plymouth local services. However, the stories which really hit the headlines related to four Royal Blue Coaches and one Black & White (Associated Motorways) vehicle.

Vehicle 2254, driver W. H. Hancock, working the 2.0 pm Bournemouth–Kingsbridge service, was stranded in snowdrifts at Winterbourne Abbas, between Dorchester and Bridport. The twenty passengers were taken off and accommodated in the village school and the Coach & Horses Inn; emergency food supplies arrived on 30 December and the next day, the coach and passengers were recovered by snowplough. Two factors stand out amid the difficulties and privations of this winter : the kindness and unstinted help given by local people where coaches became stranded and the untiring efforts made by the coach drivers concerned, who immediately accepted responsibility for the safety of their passengers and willingly took up burdens quite beyond the call of normal duties. In these real emergencies there were few complaints but only help from all sides, coupled with a ready understanding of the grave difficulties confronting the coach services. An extract from the report of Driver Hancock makes fascinating reading and dramatically illustrates these two features :

> I became stuck on the icy surface at the top of Three Sisters Hill and remained immobile at this point for 3 hours, after which I was towed out by a Matador snow-plough and proceeded to the bottom of Long Bredy Hill. I turned round on the advice of an A.A. patrol, to attempt to return to Dorchester : the driver of the snow-plough hooked his chain to the front of the coach and we proceeded up the hill towards Dorchester. From the top of the hill I proceeded on my own to Winterbourne Abbas, where after contacting Bournemouth by 'phone, it was decided that we should stay in the village, for the safety of the coach and passengers. I made my way to the Coach & Horses Inn and told my passengers I would find out the position regarding accommodation. The landlord was very nice about it and told me to bring the people in out of the cold : I got everyone inside where there was a fire and plenty of warming drinks. We then discussed accommodation and the landlord said he had 6 beds available : it was decided among the passengers that the most deserving cases should have the beds, the rest sleeping in the lounge. Later in the evening, the owner of the village store, sent her husband to say she could put up 5 more. Next morning I was at this lady's store having tea, when she informed me that she could put up the rest of the people in beds that night : so on Sunday everyone was in bed.
>
> On Monday afternoon I was informed by the local police officer that the way was open to Dorchester : I went and informed the passengers that I was leaving at 2.45—this was greeted with loud cheers. I left for

Dorchester via Martinstown; it was a rough ride but we arrived in Dorchester at 3.40, and the passengers were cleared on alternative coaches.

A more serious position developed with vehicle 1357 (Driver M. Rowe) working the 1.0 pm Exeter–Bournemouth, which had been diverted via Yeovil, together with Black & White coach (Driver Hughes) working the 3.30 pm Cheltenham–Weymouth. Both vehicles became stuck in snowdrifts on Wardon Hill, midway between Dorchester and Yeovil, at an altitude of 780 ft. The only nearby building was the Clay Pigeon Café and into this forty-two Royal Blue passengers (including seven children) plus twenty-seven Associated Motorways passengers (four children), crowded for refuge. A few elected to stay in the coaches but as conditions deteriorated, the police gave instructions that they must be taken into the café; things were so bad that one 69-year-old man was buried up to the armpits as he struggled to reach the café and had to be searched for with torches. Finally a Land-Rover from a nearby farm was pressed into service to take people from coach to café. As can be imagined with so many people (including elderly folk, small children, a 5-week-old baby and a spastic child) trying to eat, sleep and live for several days in such a confined space, matters worsened rapidly, especially as all toilet and washing facilities were frozen.

Milk for the tiny baby was on the point of running out, when a policeman on skis got through to the café on 30 December. On 31 December a doctor struggled through to the café and sent out an immediate warning, 'These people must be got out without delay'. Three naval helicopters were summoned and the nineteen worst cases were ferried by air to hospital—surely the first case in the history of road passenger transport where the Search & Rescue Service had to be brought into operation! The remaining people were rescued by army and police half-track vehicles and taken across country to Cattistock, where two coaches ferried them to Dorchester rest-centre.

The third incident involved vehicle 2203 (Driver W. C. Lynn) working the 2.30 pm Cheltenham–Bournemouth duplicate, which became stuck in snowdrifts near East Knoyle in Wiltshire.

Twenty-five passengers (including five children) were rescued by jeep and taken $1\frac{1}{2}$ miles to the Seymour Arms and other houses in the village, where they stayed for two days. As the police intimated that this road was low on their priority list for clearance, the passengers were finally taken over the fields by jeep to Semley Railway Station, where their coach tickets were exchanged for rail tickets. The coach itself could not be cleared and taken to Bournemouth until the following Saturday.

The fourth incident was less serious and of shorter duration: vehicle 1360 (Driver Richards) working the London–Plymouth service lodged in a snowdrift at Lee Mill, between Ivybridge and Plympton. It was joined shortly after by a Triumph coach carrying naval ratings from Portsmouth to Plymouth. The lights and heating system of the latter vehicle failed and its passengers, together with stray motorists also stranded, spent the night in the Royal Blue coach; the driver was able to keep the engine running, to provide light and heat. Next morning, police vehicles from Plympton reached the spot and shuttled the passengers into Plympton, where another coach toured Plymouth, dropping people at their doors.

The phenomenal weather represented a severe loss to Royal Blue: not only were passengers and revenue forfeited due to cancellation of services but many passengers, already booked, had to be transferred to British Railways or given a refund on their tickets. In addition, the company felt in duty bound to recompense all who had come to the rescue of the snowbound coaches, including a grant towards a burnt-out clutch on one of the Land-Rovers. The company also incurred abnormal maintenance and repair costs arising from damage sustained by coaches on ice-bound roads.

Personal letters were sent by the general manager to the drivers of the three vehicles stranded for two days, commending them on their initiative and the thought they had shown for passengers. There were also many testimonies from the passengers themselves and one such letter ran as follows:

My wife and I were included in the party which was stranded at the Clay Pigeon Café, when the Exeter–Bournemouth coach was unable to proceed. We should like to convey to you our very great appreciation of the way in which your driver acted throughout this emergency and his unsparing attention to the needs of his passengers without thought of himself. We noticed that during the 41 hours we were captive he had practically no sleep as he was constantly checking that everything was in order. Even during the rescue operation he actively engaged in arranging signals for the helicopter and ensuring that everything was going to plan.

We feel that such unselfish devotion to duty should not go un-noticed. . . . We also wish to thank the Company for the actions it took and realise that the stranding of the coach occurred despite all efforts to find a way through.

On 31 December 1962, only the London–Bristol service was able to operate but this had to cease the next day. One of the features of this extraordinary winter was that temperatures remained at, or below, freezing point for a full six weeks, so that any further precipitation during this period fell as snow and any slight thaws in sunshine invariably froze again overnight. Royal Blue was, therefore, confronted with a series of setbacks extending into February 1963, though none was as serious as the initial blizzard. During the night of 3-4 January, hours of heavy snow fell on Exmoor and the columns of the *Western Morning News* make incredible reading: drifts 60 ft deep in places, the tops carved and curled into fantastic shapes by the strong winds.

The daily papers reached Hartland by sledge. Gradually, routes or sections of routes were resumed, as the county councils brought snowploughs into operation and roads were shovelled clear of ice and gritted. By 9 January only three main sections could not be worked, Ilfracombe–Bournemouth, Exmouth–Bournemouth, and Yeovil–Salisbury. But on 10 January, new drifts 5-6 ft deep blocked main roads in the Tavistock and Okehampton areas and Royal Blue took another step backwards, since none of the Cornwall services could reach Exeter. There was little change in the next ten days except that the Bournemouth–Exmouth route was reopened on 12 January, but on 20 January further snow and icing caused the cancellation or curtailment of thirty journeys, including eight on the London–Bournemouth road and three on the Bournemouth–Portsmouth road, both of which had been working with little trouble since 4 January. The 5.0 pm Bournemouth–Plymouth coach became stranded late at night near Starcross (between Exeter and Dawlish) and passengers took refuge for the night in the nearby mental hospital; they were well looked after and all were allowed out next day! The Cornwall–Exeter services were snowed up at Okehampton and passengers had to spend the night in the Brandize Park Hotel.

This time, conditions improved more rapidly and by 23 January, Royal Blue was almost back to normal—until the next snow-blanket on 4 February. After 3 ft of snow, fifteen journeys were lost: Exmouth–Bournemouth was cancelled again, the Plymouth–London road was blocked at Windwhistle near Crewkerne, and the Exeter–Cornwall services could not operate. On 6 February a further blizzard struck the west country: three trains were snowed up on the Exeter–Okehampton–Tavistock line and again there were reports of 20 ft drifts on Exmoor, with gale-force winds.

Twenty-seven Royal Blue journeys were cancelled or curtailed and even the London–Bournemouth and London–Bristol routes lost certain journeys. The blizzard was followed by a sudden thaw on 7 February and widespread flooding added to the trials and hazards of travel in the South-west; twelve Royal Blue journeys had to be cancelled. Exmoor, which had suffered most throughout this extraordinary period, was subjected to a further snowfall on 10 February before the iron grip of winter started to relax. There was also a final display of snow in Cornwall on 19 February, though not enough to cause serious dislocation.

By 15 February, Royal Blue operations were practically normal and it could at last be said that the most dreadful winter in living memory was over. Local buses on some of the more remote Exmoor roads finally returned to normal operation on 14 March.

As can well be imagined, Royal Blue are extensive users of the telephone, making hundreds of long-distance calls each week. In such a winter the demands on the telephone system became even greater and more vital. During the blizzard, with motorists stranded all over the countryside, telephone lines became terribly congested. Nevertheless, the telephone authorities quickly appreciated the special needs of Royal Blue and authorised priority in the necessary cases, both from the company's offices and from the homes of senior traffic officers.

It is unusual in these days for tribute to be paid to the telephone service, who are more often the butt for criticisms, nevertheless in peace and war, Royal Blue has always found this vital communication service functioning at a very high level of efficiency.

STRANGE HAPPENINGS

By reason of its direct contact with all sections of the community, the transport industry is always in the public eye. It is perhaps the one industry that everyone, from schoolboys down to university theorists and politicians, feels fully qualified to run. Yet, in reality, it is also the one industry where practicalities and first-hand experience count for so much and theory can do so little. A firm of efficiency experts, called in a few years ago by Western/Southern National, conceded, after being given all the facts, that, within the restrictions imposed by legislation and trade union practice, they could make no suggestions whatever.

The traction units employed in the transport industry, be they steam, diesel, petrol, or electricity, by reason of their power and size fascinate children of all ages. There cannot be one transport undertaking in the country which does not possess its file of oddities, strange happenings, and weird suggestions. Royal Blue is no exception, ranging from the dear old lady who, having seen the agency supervisor's van painted in Royal Blue livery, wrote to ask if she could book a seat and 'Could I please travel in the little private coach, which follows on behind the big ones', to the odd 'case' who confessed a fascination for buses and could he please bring his sleeping-bag and bed down with the vehicles in the garage. Yet, strange as this odd correspondence is, it could hardly seem less likely than the incident concerning a dour Scot, who at last forsook his native glen and decided to launch out on a holiday in the south of France, via coach to London, and thence by air to Toulouse. He was found one morning wandering about Victoria Coach Station by a Royal Blue driver, who, ever willing to help, asked 'Where are you for?' The reply consisted of two thick monosyllables, 'Tew-lew'. 'Ah', said the driver, 'to Looe—you're just in time: put your bags here and jump in this coach, which is just starting'. And it was well beyond Hartley Wintney before it dawned upon the unfortunate traveller that, far from being on an airport coach bound for Toulouse, he was being whisked away into Cornwall. The poor man had his holiday in the south of France, though he arrived several days later than planned.

Another surprising incident took place in the Hartley Wintney area, when, on pulling up for a refreshment stop, the Royal Blue coach was boarded by police who proceeded to arrest an inoffensive looking passenger, who was in fact a long-term prisoner making his getaway by Royal Blue!

How much a trade-name and a reputation means in the eyes of the public may be judged from the letters which have been received in the vein, 'I booked a seat on Royal Blue but to my disappointment was made to travel on a Western National vehicle, not nearly so pleasant or comfortable'; in fact, the vehicle in question has often proved to be of identical design to a Royal Blue coach but painted green and cream instead of dark blue! The latest policy of Western/Southern National of painting all new intakes into their coach fleet dark blue is psychologically a very sound move. This type of complaint reached its ultimate when a letter was received complaining about the poor services provided by Western National and exhorting the management to take a leaf out of the book of the adjacent Southern National, whose services were so well organised.

An improbable but true incident, which reflected little credit on the alertness of either the passenger or the Royal Blue staff, arose when a traveller handed up his wireless licence in mistake for his coach ticket—it was accepted without demur. Correspondence ensued.

A more serious incident occurred at Salisbury, where a coach drew up for a refreshment halt. A very young girl passenger disappeared into the 'Ladies' and re-emerged fifteen minutes later—with a new-born baby, to the utter consternation of her appalled parents.

And so the file of strange occurrences goes on—encounters between coaches and motorists, vociferous as rooks mobbing an eagle, embarrassing outbursts from tipsy passengers, and the occasional letter of praise and thanks.

POST-WAR TRAFFIC TRENDS

A few words must be said about the general pattern of Royal Blue traffic since services recommenced in 1946. It is fairly common knowledge that with the abolition of petrol rationing in 1950 and the subsequent growth of private car ownership, normal bus traffic has declined by 3-4 per cent every year since. The annual passenger figures for Royal Blue since 1951, however, are as follows:

1951	1,240,305	1957	1,096,989	1963	1,526,049
1952	1,265,839	1958	1,168,435	1964	1,528,927
1953	1,305,560	1959	1,159,416	1965	1,556,038
1954	1,298,864	1960	1,277,196	1966	1,510,878
1955	1,375,472	1961	1,347,506	1967	1,471,226
1956	1,411,027	1962	1,428,946	1968	1,426,211

These figures show a slow but steady increase in traffic from 1951 to 1956, followed by a severe setback in 1957 resulting from the Suez Crisis early in the year and the disastrous national strike of bus and coach crews during the peak of the summer season. The 1957 figure stands as a grim warning of the susceptibility of passenger transport to adverse political events and the long-term damage that can be done to goodwill by precipitate industrial disputes. It took Royal Blue until 1962 to recover from these setbacks; an example, in a small way, of how easily a nation's industry can be dampened by unpropitious climates. From 1962 the passenger figures climbed steadily until the peak year 1965, when traffic was 25 per cent above the 1951 level. During the last two years there have been declines in traffic,

which can largely be attributed to two factors : first, the hand-
ing over of the Royal Blue interest in the London–Bristol–
Weston-super-Mare road to the Bristol Omnibus Co Ltd in
October 1965; and secondly, the Waterloo–Bournemouth
electrification scheme introduced by the Southern Region of
British Railways in June 1967—undoubtedly taking traffic from
the London–Bournemouth and Bournemouth–Southampton
routes of Royal Blue. If these two factors are discounted, the
remaining Royal Blue routes continue to show a buoyant traffic
trend, particularly marked on the London–Plymouth service.
The alteration of the August Bank Holiday date has affected the
spread of traffic for the past four years, in that the marked
decline of the August peak has been compensated for by significant increases at the beginning and end of the season.

There seems to be a growing awareness among the travelling
public that the inflexible fortnight, orientated around the old
August Bank Holiday, left much to be desired and that early
or late holidays have a great deal to offer, not least being a
better weather record.

Special circumstances have maintained and increased Royal
Blue traffic, contrary to normal trends in the passenger transport
industry. First, there is the enhanced spending capacity of
people in the large centres of population, notably London and
the Midlands, which has brought West-country holidays within
the range of an increasing number of people during the post-
war years : 21 per cent of the total United Kingdom tourist
traffic now visits the South-west each year. This increased spending power has more than balanced the effect of private-car
ownership, though it is doubtful whether this trend can be continued so markedly in future years, unless private motoring
becomes a more difficult proposition or foreign holidays become
too expensive. Secondly, there is the increased comfort and
dependability of coach travel in the post-war years, which have
undoubtedly led to a significant increase in middle-aged and
elderly passengers—people who do not wish to be bothered with
the alarms and trials of modern motoring and to whom journey
time is not a vital factor. To these people, the comparatively

cheap fares offered by coach travel, coupled with direct transport to the centre of the town they are visiting, count for more than the saving of an hour or two. Thirdly, Royal Blue must thank British Railways for a certain amount of additional traffic, as a result of the inevitable closure of branch lines in the South-west, particularly since 1960.

Finally, perhaps Royal Blue can make some claim to good and progressive management, particularly in supplying the needs of the cross-country traveller, and the inhabitants of the outer London suburbs and satellite towns. New services have been provided from these outlying residential areas direct to the South-west, while the linking of facilities with 'Eastern National', Maidstone & District, and other companies, has ensured through operation from the expanding areas of the South-east direct to the resorts of Devon and Cornwall. Moreover, the retention and increase of traffic over the years, has enabled fares to be kept at a reasonable level (most journeys are still at the low rate of about 2d per mile). It is a well known fact, brought out at several hearings before the traffic commissioners, that the Royal Blue express services assist financially to some extent in the maintenance of the stage carriage facilities of Western & Southern National, which would otherwise be operating at a financial loss. Many local residents in remote hamlets in Devon, Cornwall, Somerset, and Dorset owe the continuation of their local bus services at the present level of both frequency and fares, to the coaches which daily ply the roads to distant destinations in the eastern and midland counties.

FARES

Nevertheless, Royal Blue fares have had to rise in our inflationary economy. Before the Second World War there was no fixed method of calculating fares; they were determined by the cut and thrust of commercial considerations and differed in rate per mile for every route. A rough average of 1d per mile would not be far from the mark. During the post-war years, most bus companies have gradually brought their fares on to a mileage

K

scale, the rate per mile generally decreasing with the distance travelled. This process has not been so easy for Royal Blue, with routes strung across the whole of south England, many of them shared for part of their length with other express service operators. Until 1968, it did not prove practicable to formulate a mileage scale which would be acceptable to all the other operators concerned and at the same time maintain Royal Blue revenue between principal destinations at an equitable level. The successive changes in fares since 1945 have been as follows:

1946 Pre-war fares raised by 16 2/3 per cent, when Royal Blue services recommenced after the war.
1950 All fares raised by 7 1/7 per cent.
1952 All fares raised by 6 2/3 per cent.
1956 Fares applicable on Fri nights, Sats, and Suns during the Summer months increased by 12½ per cent in an endeavour to move traffic away from the busy summer weekends.
1957 Basic fares increased by 5 per cent. Fri night/Sat fares fixed at 22½ per cent above basic rate and Sun fares at 12½ per cent above basic rate.
1960 Basic fares increased by 8¼ per cent, with Fri night/Sat fares remaining at 22½ per cent above basic rate. Sun fares returned to normal basic rate, as it was found no longer necessary to discourage Sun travel.
1961 All fares raised by 8¼ per cent.
1963 All fares raised by 8¼ per cent.
1965 Basic fares increased by 5 per cent but day return fares left unchanged. Fri night/Sat fares increased by 8¼ per cent.
1966 All fares raised by 8¼ per cent.
1968 Basic fares revised on a mileage scale (with certain limitations), except on routes out of London common with other operators. Rates: Single Fares: 2¼d per mile. Period Return Fares: 2d per mile. Day Return Fares (where existing): 1.18d per mile. Fri night/Sat fares calculated at 27 per cent above basic fares.
1969 Basic fares on an amended mileage scale, viz—Single Fares: 2.3625d per mile. Period Return Fares: 2.1d per mile. Day Return Fares (where existing): 1.24d per mile. Fri night/Sat fares at 25 per cent above basic fares.

What do these successive fare increases add up to? They mean, in effect, that basic fares are a little more than double and Friday night/Saturday fares are about 2½ times pre-war.

There can be few other articles which have only doubled in price since 1939 and it is worth considering some of the factors which have enabled fares to be held down, in the face of operating costs some four times as great as the 1939 level.

1. Increased seating capacity has resulted in greater productivity from each vehicle. The seating capacity of coaches in 1939 was 32·6, compared with 39 in 1963, while during 1964 fourteen new RELH vehicles with 45 seats were taken into the fleet. The latest 45-seater, compared with the largest pre-war vehicle seating 36, represents a 25 per cent increase in passenger seats and to that extent duplicate vehicles and the employment of extra crews can be reduced.

2. The change-over of the entire fleet to diesel propulsion in 1954 gave a greater mileage per gallon of fuel and an increased engine-life with fewer vehicles out of service for mechanical reasons.

3. The progressive introduction of night services has resulted in a spread of traffic and more consistent vehicle usage. The vehicle performing a night journey from London to Plymouth, for instance, is available for a return load from Plymouth to London next morning: its work-output is doubled.

4. The growth of traffic generally has helped to offset the need for fare increases, assisted no doubt by the amenities of modern vehicles—air conditioning, heating, improved springing, and reduced engine-noise from the under-floor or rear-engine positions.

5. The raising of the speed limit for passenger vehicles from 30 mph to 40 mph in 1961, and to 50 mph in 1966, also helped to improve the efficiency of operation. While the higher speed limits have been somewhat offset by increasing traffic congestion, certain reductions in running times have taken place, eg London–Bournemouth has been cut by about 20 min. Fully loaded non-stop duplicate coaches are also able to proceed on their journeys more expeditiously, without the irksome necessity for holding speed down below the capabilities of modern engines.

6. The removal or relaxation of irritating booking restrictions has also helped to make the services available to many 'last-minute' passengers. It is now the policy of Royal Blue to accept unbooked, on-the-spot, passengers whenever accommodation permits, and drivers are allowed to issue tickets to any such casual travellers.

7. The use of modern techniques has also played its part, notably the employment of the Telex System, installed at Bournemouth in 1964 and Exeter in 1969. This has enabled the instant transmission and reception of information by teleprinter and has contributed to the most efficient usage of vehicles and staff. A similar machine has been installed by London Coastal Coaches at Victoria Coach Station, which Royal Blue is able to use.

THE PROBLEM OF THE SUMMER SATURDAY

In spite of all publicity and efforts to spread holidays, the English habit of taking holidays from Saturday to Saturday is little changed and since many people's vacations are also dictated by the dates of school holidays, there are inevitable peaks on Saturdays during July and August. How does Royal Blue cope with these peaks, when passenger traffic can expand to three or four times the normal volume? It is here that the advantages of being an integral part of a large omnibus undertaking come into play, for apart from the fleet of 116 Royal Blue coaches, Western & Southern National possess a further 134 coaches, which are normally employed on excursions, tours, and private hire work. Since most holidaymakers are in the process of travelling to and from the resorts on Saturdays, the need for local tours is almost non-existent on that day, and a bare minimum of private hire work is accepted at higher rates than normal. This means that, with most of the Western & Southern National Coach fleet available to it Royal Blue can double its fleet on summer Saturdays. Even this is not sufficient for the really busy Saturdays, so approaches are first made to neighbouring associated companies, who have tours coaches to spare on Saturdays— Devon General (Grey Cars), Greenslades Tours, Hants & Dorset Motor Services, and Wilts & Dorset Motor Services. These companies have very few express service commitments themselves and their coaches may be seen on summer Saturdays operating Royal Blue express services.

By this means the available fleet is swelled still further, but even these resources are not enough for the busiest Saturdays. So finally, Royal Blue turns to the smaller local operators for spare coaches. An official hiring list is kept and the operator's vehicles are inspected, before his name is placed on the list, to ensure that the vehicles chosen measure up to the required standard for long-distance coach travel. On a Saturday in August it is quite an experience to visit a main interchange point, for example Exeter coach station : vehicles of all colours and makes can be seen, drivers in all types of uniform, crowds of passengers of all ages and sizes, and little islands of stacked luggage. One wonders how it can all be sorted out, but the Royal Blue inspectors are experienced and efficient and it is very rare indeed for a passenger to board the wrong coach or find his luggage despatched to a different destination from himself. The holiday atmosphere pervades the scene and there is quite a 'carnival' air about it all.

The spread of the holiday season away from the old August

Bank Holiday has helped in the past few years, but it is still common for several hundred coaches to be in operation on Royal Blue journeys on a peak Saturday. Many vehicles can achieve good loads in both directions—down from the population centres to the South-west with people starting their holidays, back with people finishing their holidays—even so after a busy Saturday there is the inevitable balance of coaches which have to return empty to their home depot, often over 100 miles away. So, those passengers who may be tempted to think that Royal Blue must be making large profits, if only for the government, should consider what may be the movements of their vehicle and driver after the service run has been completed. A full coach in one direction and an empty coach back again represents only a half load on average.

It can well be understood that the employment of vehicles and drivers from so many sources can present problems, so from 1955 onwards Royal Blue have compiled and issued a standard 'Route Detail Book'. This 100-page booklet not only contains particulars of all scheduled service routes, with complete details of streets to be used in passing through towns, but also includes separate sections covering the routes of non-stop journeys and alternative direct routes for fully loaded duplicates. There is also a section setting out routes to be followed between terminal points and garages and particulars of those Associated Motorways scheduled routes on which Royal Blue vehicles are likely to be operated. This comprehensive guide for drivers finally includes a list of towns where stopping place limitations apply, together with details of these stops.

BOOKING AND CHARTING PROCEDURE

The reader may be interested to know what happens between the time when a passenger walks into a booking agent's or company's office to buy a coach ticket and when he boards the vehicle to make his journey.

The ticket, blue for a single or forward journey and red for a return journey, is made out in triplicate. The passenger receives the top copy, the second or confirmation copy is posted off to the relevant charting office, and the third or audit copy remains in the ticket book. The Royal Blue charting offices are located at Bournemouth, London, Exeter, and Taunton; and there the confirmation copies of tickets are sorted out and recorded on charts for each journey. A typical chart is reproduced here.

A.M. P.M.	ILFRACOMBE – BOURNEMOUTH VIA MINEHEAD		DATE			
PICK–UP	PASSENGERS ON	SET DOWN	CHELTENHAM	LONDON	H·WYC·	MAX PASS
ILFRACOMBE						
COMBE MARTIN						
LYNTON						
SIMONSBATH						
EXFORD						
DUNSTER						
MINEHEAD						
CARHAMPTON						
WASHFORD						
WILLITON						
BRIDGWATER	TRANSFERS					
BRIDGWATER						
LANGPORT						
SOMERTON						
MARTOCK						
ILMINSTER						
STOKE–S–HAMB.						
MONTACUTE						
HOUNDSTONE C.						
YEOVIL						
SHERBORNE						
N. WOOTTON						
BISHOPS CAUNDLE						
LYDLINCH						
STUR. NEWTON						
SHILLINGSTONE						
BLANDFORD						
CHARLTON MARSH						
SPETISBURY						
WIMBORNE						
POOLE						
PARKSTONE						
BOURNEMOUTH						

Specimen booking chart

As bookings come in, the cumulative total of passengers to be picked up is entered in the squares under the 'Passengers On' column against each picking-up point. At transfer points (Bridgwater on the above chart) the number of passengers to be transferred is segregated on to the separate line provided. The set-down points are dealt with similarly on the right-hand side of the chart. By this method every passenger is guaranteed a seat and the charts show the company the number of travellers from each point and how many vehicles will be required to accommodate them. If more than one charting office is involved in a booking, the confirmation copy of the ticket is endorsed 'charted at . . .' and passed to the other office. Before the journey, an instruction envelope is compiled for the driver with the information collected from the charts. The envelope gives details of the number of passengers to be picked up and set down at each point, and also serves as a waybill, mileage record, and mechanical report. Tickets are collected from passengers by the driver, placed in the envelope, and returned to the company—the wheel has turned full circle.

When a passenger books a return ticket, it is not essential for him to say when the return portion will be used; he may go to any agent and have the date inserted or adjusted later. The agent for his part has a special 'Charting Details Form for Open Dated or Altered Tickets' for recording the alteration, which he forwards to the relevant charting office.

The audit copy of the ticket speaks for itself : it enables the cash due from an agent or office to be checked against the tickets issued. Royal Blue has some 350 agents in its territory and to help them carry out the correct procedures quickly and in standard form, a 30-page instruction book for agents is issued. This covers every possible contingency from, 'Dogs & Household Pets—Dogs must be crated for journeys by air', to lost tickets and bookings for Europabus Services to all parts of the continent. A table of routes or sections of routes, with the appropriate charting office to which confirmation copies of tickets must be sent, is of course included. To look after all these booking agents, Royal Blue has an agency supervisor, whose duties are to travel round the various booking offices to audit ticket issues, supply timetables and publicity matter, explain any new facilities or procedures, follow up any complaints, and generally act as liaison between the company and its agents. Not all companies operating express services employ supervisors but there is no doubt that the periodic calls and special visits to iron out particular problems are of great value to the agents and to the company.

This brief account of the intricate internal machinery behind booking a ticket may perhaps cause the passenger to blush next time he decides at the last minute to return home by the 10.30 am instead of the 4.30 pm because the weather looks nasty. Nevertheless, every effort is made to help the passenger faced with sudden contingencies and provided the coach is not booked to capacity, no random passenger is refused. This may 'upset the system' slightly but Royal Blue exists to serve the traveller, and the policy of accepting on-the-spot passengers has contributed to a marked increase in off-peak traffic.

RAIL CLOSURES

Railway line closures are no new thing in the South-west; they were taking place in a desultory fashion over thirty years ago (eg the Barnstaple–Lynton narrow-gauge line in 1935). The whole process, however, has been speeded up in the post-war years and placed very much in the limelight by the Beeching Report of 1963. Perhaps it is not surprising that the western counties, with their sparse population and scant industrial activity, should have incurred more railway closures than many other parts of Great Britain. A note of some of the lines and stations closed to passenger traffic, adjacent to Royal Blue routes, since 1945, is contained in Appendix H.

It is difficult to estimate the effects of all these closures on Royal Blue traffic, since in no cases were Royal Blue specifically ordered by the Minister to provide additional journeys or services in substitution for rail facilities. Associated Motorways, however, were involved in the provision of a new service in 1966, when the Somerset & Dorset Line closed: the Minister, in approving closure, ordered the operation of two express journeys per day between Bristol and Bournemouth via Bath, Radstock, Shepton Mallet, Wincanton, Stalbridge, Sturminster Newton, Blandford, and Poole. This service is still in operation.

Nevertheless, it cannot be doubted that the cumulative effect of the withdrawal of so many rail facilities has tended to produce more passengers on Royal Blue routes. It is interesting to note that with the withdrawal of rail branch services linking with the main line, Royal Blue can offer faster facilities over quite considerable distances, eg Bude–Exeter, Perranporth–Exeter, and Exeter–Bournemouth. On routes cutting across the main rail network, the time saving can be far greater, coach services often providing the only feasible alternative. Many passengers, particularly those to whom time is not the most pressing factor, prefer to travel by coach from London, for instance, direct to the centre of the resort they are visiting, rather than by train to railheads, with subsequent local bus journeys to the resorts. In particular, as rail services have concentrated increasingly on trunk routes, more and more people have turned to Royal Blue for cross-country journeys, away from the rail network: Bournemouth–Exeter and Bournemouth–Ilfracombe are good examples. Royal Blue, ever on the lookout for new traffic, has introduced various revised or additional services which can be said to be the direct result of rail closures. These have all been done purely as commercial ventures, without direction or subsidisation, in an effort to build up traffic. Examples are

1. Tiverton–Taunton: one journey daily in each direction, linking at Taunton with the main express service network to London, the Midlands, etc. These journeys were introduced in 1963, but after operation for 2½ years, the service did not prove a commercial success and was withdrawn.

2. Taunton–Barnstaple–Ilfracombe: one additional journey daily in each direction during the summer months was introduced in 1964 in anticipation of the closure of the Taunton–Barnstaple railway line. This also proved unsuccessful and was withdrawn after 2½ years' operation. However, a further experiment with an additional daily journey in each direction during the winter months was tried in 1967 and is still working.

3. Bude–Exeter: a new service of one journey per day in each direction was introduced for the summer of 1966 in view of the closure of the Okehampton–Bude railway line. This facility was repeated for summer 1967 (Easter to mid-October) and extended to operate throughout the year from Easter 1968. In view of this new service, the existing Taunton–Ilfracombe–Bude route was truncated at Westward Ho!

4. Bournemouth–Exmouth: an additional daily journey in each direction was introduced during the summer months in 1964, as a result of the closure, or pending closure, of various rail branch lines in East Devon and South Dorset. This proved an unsuccessful venture and was withdrawn after two summers.

5. Inter-availability of stage and express service tickets was introduced between Taunton–Yeovil and Newquay–Perranporth following rail

closures, in order to offer the public the fullest use of available road facilities.

Too much stress should not be placed on rail closures, however, as the traffic directly accruing from them has proved very small indeed in the experience of Western/Southern National. They are just one factor among many which have helped to maintain the level of Royal Blue passengers.

STRUCTURE, MANAGEMENT, AND MAINTENANCE OF VEHICLES

Policy and general management are carried out from the Exeter headquarters of Western/Southern National, who are the licence holders for all express routes. The day-to-day running and control of services is in the hands of a traffic superintendent at Bournemouth, with inspectors at London, Exeter, Salisbury, Bournemouth, and Portsmouth. These inspectors have local control of services and any driving staff based on their centres. About one-third of the Royal Blue fleet, however, is based on Western National and Southern National depots, manned by National staff, who interwork both stage and express services. The current allocation of Royal Blue vehicles is given in Appendix E.

On the maintenance side, there is an area engineer at Rutland Road Depot, Bournemouth.

All Royal Blue coaches are give a regular weekly check and are overhauled on a mileage basis. The vehicles pass through a docking procedure at Bournemouth or Plymouth every 75,000 miles and each fourth dock is regarded as a major overhaul, undertaken at the Western National main workshops at Plymouth: engine, gearbox, differential, front axle, steering box, and other mechanical and electrical components are stripped, repaired, and renewed where necessary. The average annual mileage of a Royal Blue coach is 58,000 and during its lifetime each coach runs some 600,000 miles. The total Royal Blue fleet covers some 5,000,000 miles annually.

During the last ten years, in order to keep booking agents in touch with the increasing complexity of express services, agency conferences have been held at least once per year. Different centres are chosen for each conference, which affords valuable opportunities for agents to meet the Royal Blue management personally and discuss mutual problems.

PUBLICITY

From 1946 onward, Royal Blue have issued a comprehensive timetable book for all express coach services and the latest summer issue comprises 100 pages for the very modest price of 9d. From October 1965 the separate timetable leaflets for each route were abandoned and replaced by four neat area folders for which no charge is made:

1. All services to and from London.
2. All services to and from North Devon & Somerset.
3. All services to and from South Devon & Cornwall.
4. All services to and from Hampshire and the South Coast.

These area folders have greatly simplified the work of agents and the answering of enquiries generally, besides affording members of the public more comprehensive information than the individual route leaflets. Special posters are issued to draw attention to new facilities or major changes, accompanied by Press publicity.

Pictorial posters and show cards, advertising express coach travel generally, are provided for display both in companies' offices and at agents' premises and a standard metal Royal Blue board is placed outside agencies. Special illuminated box-signs may also be seen in some office windows.

Full details of all Royal Blue services also appear in the *ABC Coach & Bus Guide*, a 500-page, 10s od (50p) publication, which covers all coach services and longer-distance bus services throughout England, Scotland and Wales.

REFRESHMENT HALTS

This is a perennial problem. People travelling long distances by coach must have periodic halts for refreshment, which means that they descend in bulk on a café and all require serving with a minimum of delay, often at odd times of the day or even the night. There is no perfect solution to the difficulty, though the advent of the self-service café has greatly helped. Things were at their worst just after the Second World War and the Royal Blue management spent a great deal of time in frantic searches for premises that could meet even the minimum requirements of coach passengers. The best answer lies in the café within the modern coach station, leased to caterers who understand coach requirements, and under continual surveillance from the operator to ensure reasonable standards. Such refreshment rooms now exist at Exeter, Basingstoke, Bournemouth, Bridgwater, Bridport, Salisbury, and Winchester, but there are still some doubtful premises where things are not all that could be desired.

CHAPTER TEN

THE ROLLING STOCK

FIRST VENTURES

IN Chapters 1 and 2 we mentioned the horse-drawn vehicles and early motor cars operated by Elliotts, but we now intend to summarise the development of the rolling stock, ranging from the first char-a-bancs to the present day coaches. The fleet list (Appendix A) and the other appendices set out a large amount of detailed information regarding Royal Blue vehicles.

For coach-touring the first motor coaches were in fact char-a-bancs, which, except for a few preserved examples, have now disappeared from the transport scene. By definition the char-a-banc is a long open carriage with transverse seats, but in practice, once the earlier horse-drawn char-a-bancs had been replaced by motor vehicles, it was usual to have folding hoods which, in later years, were supplemented by celluloid side screens slotted into the bodywork. Along the nearside of the body was a row of doors, each giving access to a row of seats. In many instances a false door was panelled on the offside to match. The seats were high off the ground as the low-slung chassis had not been developed at that time, and solid tyres were the order of the day. Another feature was a running board and it was usual to carry a pair of wooden steps to assist passengers in boarding.

After the First World War, improved char-a-bancs with pneumatic tyres, a door at the front and rear with a centre gangway, and other mechanical improvements, were put into service. Various types of hood were tried, together with side-window frames, and from this there developed the coach body with sliding roof on a low-slung chassis that ousted the char-a-banc towards the end of the 1920s.

Elliotts' first two char-a-bancs were Dennis 28 hp vehicles, registered on 20 March 1913. From this early start Elliotts always referred to their vehicles as motor coaches. In the same year the Dennis vehicles were joined by a Daimler, which was followed by four others in 1914. A batch of six Seldens came in 1915 together with two secondhand De Dions, one of which (EL 1718) was later sold and converted to a lorry. A further nine Seldens were purchased in 1916 but due to the war no further vehicles were available until 1919, when the fleet was strengthened by the arrival of six AECs and seventeen 30 hp Daimlers. When subsequently withdrawn from service and sold, a number of these vehicles saw further service after conversion to lorries.

POST 1918 BUILD-UP

It is unfortunate that detailed records do not exist of all the vehicles acquired by Elliott Bros during the period from 1923 to the first half of 1928. However, the authors believe that the details in Appendix A include all public service vehicles owned with the exception of three Daimler 'Y' types and one Daimler 'CK' type. It is thought that these four vehicles were purchased secondhand from Petter Engines of Yeovil. At the end of 1927 the firm was operating thirty-four Daimler 'Y' types fitted with 26-seater bodies, twenty Daimler 'CK' types with bodies of 14 to 26 seating capacity (presumably char-a-bancs) and eighteen AEC 26-seater coaches.

Char-a-banc bodies for Elliott Bros coaches were built by Branksome Carriage Works, Randsome Body Builders, Steanes, Grahame White, London Lorries Ltd, and by their own staff at Norwich Avenue garage.

As a result of the agreement of 1924 between Elliott Bros and Hants & Dorset Motor Services Limited, described in Chapter 2, the twelve Daimler 'Y' types (EL 8771/2/3, EL 8900/1/2, EL 9188, EL 9385, EL 9410, CR 8636, CR 8828, and

CR 9081), which had been bodied by Dodson, did not enter service with Elliott Bros but went direct into the Hants & Dorset fleet. These vehicles had all-weather bus bodies, giant pneumatic tyres, and, though painted and lettered ready for Royal Blue, they were repainted for Hants & Dorset before being moved from the body manufacturers' premises. It is believed that these were the first pneumatic-tyred vehicles to have been operated by Hants & Dorset Motor Services Limited.

During 1926 the Associated Daimler Company was formed by a combination of the AEC and Daimler companies, and, though it was a short-lived coalition which divided in 1928 when each concern resumed independent manufacture of commercial vehicle chassis, Elliott Bros had time enough to purchase a number of ADC chassis. As previously mentioned the records for most of the period no longer exist, but early in 1928 a batch of ADC 424 vehicles with Duple coach bodies, registered RU 6711 to RU 6736 inclusive, entered the Royal Blue fleet. With the sale of the business in 1935 these were shared between Western/Southern National and Hants & Dorset, though the latter operator did not use any of them despite the fact that they were allocated fleet numbers.

Elliott Bros' next new vehicles were among the last ADCs to be built and henceforth all were of the forward control type. Although RU7730 to RU 7735 inclusive were ordered as ADC 426s with Duple bodies and delivered in July 1928 they were renamed AEC Reliances in November 1929. Two of this batch which were transferred to Hants & Dorset were not licensed or used by them and were quickly sold.

For the 1929 season Elliotts put into service twenty-five AEC Reliances and six Daimler CF6s. The Daimler CF6 was available as 'forward' or 'normal' control and it reintroduced the famous 'fluted-top' radiator which had long been a characteristic feature of their motor cars, though it had not been used on their public service vehicles for over twenty years. The CF6 was powered by a version of their $5\frac{3}{4}$ litre sleeve-valve ('Silent Knight') engine, similar to that in use in some of the large Daimler cars but derated to 100 bhp. Aluminium alloys were widely employed in the CF6 chassis, which also featured servo-assisted braking.

In Elliotts' publicity there were numerous references to their fleet of Daimler 'Silent Knights'. It is worth recording that the engine which bears this name resulted from the work in 1908 of a young engineer named Knight from Wisemain, USA who produced a new type of power unit, the legendary sleeve-valve that resulted in the sleeve-valve engine being adopted for all Daimler vehicles from 1909 onwards. It was not until the early 1930s that Daimler reverted to a conventional poppet-valve type engine.

Towards the end of 1929 an AEC Regal, a Maudslay, and a Daimler, all with Duple bodies were placed in service. The three 'independent types' came in the November and were all 1929 Earls Court Show models. It is evident that Elliott Bros were experimenting with different types.

A further experimental vehicle, Leyland TS2, LJ 875, entered the fleet in February 1930. All the vehicles delivered in 1929 and 1930 survived to be transferred in 1935 but none of the AEC Reliances acquired by Hants & Dorset were numbered, licensed, or operated by them.

The Duple bodies favoured by Elliott Bros were most luxurious, with sunshine roofs, curtains, and in most cases two entrance doors. The roof luggage containers first appeared on the Daimler CF6s and the AEC Reliances, which also sported a roof-top route indicator board. Both these features, somewhat modified and refined, were to be a feature of Royal Blue coaches for the next thirty years. Elliott Bros had a further distinctive feature on their AEC Regal and Daimler CF6 coaches, in the form of horizontal wooden beading around the lowest portion of the body panels.

The Leyland and Maudslay proved to be the 'odd men out' and new coaches for 1930 were Daimler CF6s (LJ 1501–LJ 1509 inclusive and LJ 1528–LJ 1533 inclusive) and AEC Regals (LJ 1510–LJ 1527 inclusive). These vehicles all had Duple coach bodies of varying seating capacity and the AECs had 7.4 litre petrol engines, the Regal chassis being a development of the Reliance. LJ 1528 was destroyed in an accident and written off on 14 July 1932. After the sale of the business and before 1939, the majority of these coaches transferred to Western/Southern National were rebodied by Duple or Beadle, as was one of the ADCS and some of the Reliances. LJ 1519 was severely damaged by enemy action on 11 August 1943 and was subsequently broken up by Western National.

Elliott Bros acquired six coaches with the business of Olympic Coaches (ex-Traveller Coaches) and of these five were subsequently transferred to Western/Southern National and one to Hants & Dorset Motor Services. Five were disposed of before 1939 and the Dennis Lancet (PJ 5494) was completely destroyed in 1941 as a result of enemy action whilst parked in the garage at Plymouth. The last vehicle to be acquired by Elliott Bros was AEL 495, a Leyland with a somewhat obscure history, which arrived in July 1934. Shortly before this, however, four AEC 'Q's had entered service, two in 1933 and the other two in 1934. All five (the Leyland and the AEC 'Q's) passed to Hants & Dorset in 1935.

The AEC 'Q's require special mention and Elliott Bros owned the first to be built. The chassis was of unconventional design and the AEC 7.4 litre vertical engine was located on the offside of the chassis frame behind the front axle. Access to the engine and gearbox was gained by removing detachable body panels and the transmission was taken to the offside of the rear axle, which was located well towards the rear of the chassis, giving a very short rear overhang. Large section tyres were used all round, with single rear wheels. Three of the bodies were built by Duple and one by Harrington; and seating was provided for 35 passengers except in LJ 8601 which accommodated 37. On certain of the 'Q's the luggage container was built into the roof and this, coupled with the full front, gave a streamlined appearance. Although these vehicles were used by Elliott Bros on long-distance services they were not transferred to the 'National' Companies but went to the Hants & Dorset where they were employed on excursions and tours.

L

LIVERY

Originally the first horse-drawn vehicles were painted Royal Blue, but later some were painted in a pale blue though the trading name was retained. In addition a fleet name display was used, in the form of a belt and buckle device with the initials 'TE' in the centre.

The origin of the trading name is not known, though it probably stems from the contemporary custom of distinguishing vehicles by colours. Following the use of pale blue for some of the horse-drawn vehicles, the char-a-bancs appeared so painted (though the first two were in fact painted dark—Royal—blue) and the practice of painting them pale or sky blue continued until the early 1920s when the dark blue was reintroduced. Fleet numbers, with suffix letters, were used on the char-a-bancs but this was discontinued when the fleet livery was changed. An attractive fleet name, introduced in about 1919, was displayed on the side and rear panels of the coaches, and it is interesting to note that the motto 'Pulchritudo et Salubritas' (Beauty and Health) was the same as that used on the Bournemouth Corporation coat of arms. The use of this fleet name display was also discontinued with the livery change, though the belt and buckle device with the initials EB in the centre which had always appeared on all vehicles was retained.

ROYAL BLUE – NATIONAL

When Royal Blue was sold to Thos Tilling Limited the fleet was split three ways, an equal number of vehicles going to Western National, Southern National, and Hants & Dorset. An examination of the fleet list—Appendix A—gives full details of the vehicle transfers, and perhaps the first indication of the new management was the appearance in March 1935 of Bristol JJW coaches on the London–Bournemouth service. These Bristols strengthened the fleet and came in two batches; the first, BTA 453–460 (163–170) in March 1935, had 6-cylinder

petrol engines and 32-seater Eastern Counties bodies. Number
164, when new, appeared in an experimental livery of blue with
a cream roof, but this was not continued.

The second batch, ATT 921–940 (171–190) were delivered
in August 1935, some with Beadle and others with MCW
bodies. Numbers 184 and 188 were delivered new as Southern
National coaches and did not enter the Royal Blue fleet until
August 1937. Transfers of this nature have occurred from time
to time and details are included in the fleet list.

When new, a distinguishing feature was the unpainted polished
bonnet sides and as delivered, the vehicles were painted blue
overall with a relieving cream waist-band. This was later changed
to blue, with cream for the window frames, edging and side
panels above the windows to roof level. Coaches of both batches
had 5-speed Bristol KS gearboxes and in July 1936, as an experiment, No 174 was fitted with Philco type T 1803 wireless and
individual headphones. No 186 was damaged by fire on 1 August
1940 and the body was scrapped. The chassis was left unused
until May 1947 when it received the body from No 184, which
in turn was rebodied with a new 'Beadle' bus body.

Nos 163–190 were petrol-engined coaches while in the Royal
Blue fleet but all were eventually converted to Gardner 5LW
or AEC 7.7 litre oil engines when rebodied as buses in 1948-9.
All the first batch and several of the second batch were converted during the Second World War to gas producer operation (see Chapter 6, p 95).

The seventy-one vehicles taken over from Elliott Bros were,
in the main, operated on express services but odd ones were
transferred to the Western/Southern National coach fleets.
Whilst several were rebodied and continued in service after the
war, some forty-eight were disposed of before 1939, the majority
in 1937. As replacement, further coaches were added to the
Royal Blue fleet in 1936 by way of ten 1930-built petrol-engined
Leyland Tigers purchased from the Devon General Omnibus &
Touring Co Ltd in October 1935. They were rebodied by Beadle
and those for Western National (3568–3573) were for a time
during the war engaged on troop movements. Subsequently they

were converted to gas-producer operation and did not return to civilian use until 1946-7. The other four (3574–3577) were Southern National and due to shorter overall length only had 28-seater bodies as opposed to 32 in the Western National six.

New vehicles in 1937 for Royal Blue were a batch of sixteen AEC Regals; 1050–1057 were Western National with Mumford bodies and 1058–1067 were Southern National with Duple bodies. They were all subsequently rebodied and were withdrawn in April 1957. Also placed in service in 1937 were two Southern National Leyland TS3s (2981–82) and three Western National Leyland TS2s (2863/4/6) and an ex-Tourist Leyland TS3 (3527). All were rebodied by Beadle before transfer to Royal Blue. For 1938 another Southern National coach (2794 Leyland TS1) was rebodied by Beadle and no further additions were made until 1939 when Western National Leyland TS1s (3140/1/2), Southern National Leyland TS1s (3104/5), and an ex-Tourist Leyland TS1 (3537) and AEC Regal (3540), all with new Beadle bodies, entered Royal Blue service. The twenty-three rehabilitated Leyland Tiger coaches which entered the Royal Blue fleet all had petrol engines, the last petrol-engined vehicle being 3537. This completed the vehicle position when war broke out in September 1939.

POST WAR

The first vehicles to enter service were 1200/01 which were delivered new in May 1948. During the same year thirty similar vehicles were purchased. The chassis employed represented a return to Bristol manufacture in the form of the 'L' type powered by a Bristol 8.14 litre 6-cylinder AVW oil engine for Nos 1200–24 and AEC 7.7 litre engines for Nos 1225–37. All chassis had the standard Bristol clutch and five-speed gearbox. Bodywork was by John C. Beadle (Coachbuilders) Ltd of Dartford and the design was carried out by engineers of the Western and Southern National. The body design had a 'family tree' likeness to its predecessors and represented the outcome of experience with the earlier vehicles. At the same time as these vehicles were being built, several older units received new bodies of similar design to the '1200' class. It is interesting to note that, when withdrawn, some of these vehicles were exported for service overseas.

In 1949 thirteen similar new coaches (1229–1234 and 1238–1244) were purchased but those delivered in 1950 (1245–1263), whilst of generally similar design to the earlier '1200' class, had bodies built by Duple Motor Bodies Ltd. The announcement on 11 February 1950 by the Minister of Transport that all new four-wheeled public service vehicles first registered on or after 1 June 1950 could be up to 30 ft long resulted in a change to the order for Bristol L6Bs, then being built for Royal Blue. It was decided to take advantage of the new regulations and have the vehicles built on to the lengthened chassis, thereby increasing the seating capacity. This resulted in Nos 1250–1278 being classified as Bristol LL6Bs.

Considered by many to have been one of the neatest post-war coach designs, the 'exposed radiator' class are now all withdrawn from Royal Blue service; 1200–1225 had their bodies removed and sold, chassis stripped, overhauled and reassembled, incorporating rear frame extensions. They were reclassified LL6B and one LL6A in 1958, and were rebodied by Eastern Coach Works as 39-seater front door, one-man operated buses. All were still with either Western or Southern National in August 1969. The remainder, 1226–78, have been sold or broken up.

Car 1269 now belongs to R. A. Pryor of Bournemouth, still in Royal Blue colours. With the removal of one or two seats, the installation of a table, kitchen cabinets and bunks, it is used for conveying his family and equipment to archaeological 'digs' and on holidays. During 1967 this vehicle performed, without trouble, a 4-month tour of France, including a climb to 5,000 ft in the Pyrenees; it was photographed by a reporter in Paris, unknown to the owner, who was surprised to open his newspaper next morning and find a picture and write-up of his 'outre-channel Bristol, bien âgé mais très digne'.

The next batch of vehicles, numbered 1279–92, entered service in 1952 and were of a very advanced design; the chassis

BRISTOL/ECW 'MW' up to 2269

Front elevation of MW coaches up to No 2269

was manufactured by Bristol and the body by Eastern Coach
Works, the final appearance being not unlike the AEC 'Q' of
1934 though structurally and mechanically quite different.
Known as the Bristol 'LS' chassis, the principal difference from
previous vehicles is the substantial front overhang, the driver
and controls being located ahead of the front axle. The LS is a
semi-integral constructed vehicle, much of the rigidity of the
finished unit relying on the body shell. However, the chassis can
be driven as a separate unit and with a suitable bracing member,
the journey from Bristol to the body manufacturers was made
possible.

Seating was provided for 41 persons and the roof luggage container was also built into the body, which followed the pattern
of similar bodies (roof modification excepted) brought into
service by other companies of the Tilling group. Other special
Royal Blue features included the destination indicator box and
via blind panel, but the side roller blinds, which were a feature
of the company's vehicles for so many years, were discontinued
and replaced by transparent panels on each side of the roof with
the words ROYAL BLUE COACH SERVICE. Only twenty-
four coaches of the new design retained this lettering and all
subsequent deliveries were equipped with glass quarter lights
in this position.

The Gardner 6HLW oil engine and five-speed gearbox was
used as standard. In 1960 the seating capacity was reduced to
39 and in 1967 six of the vehicles were withdrawn and sold.
When car 3537, a rebodied Leyland TS1 was withdrawn on
17 March 1954, this marked the change in the entire fleet of
Royal Blue coaches from rear entrance to front entrance.
Previous coaches having rear entrances had by then been sold
or rebodied as front entrance. All subsequent coaches have had
front-entrance position.

In 1958 the LS chassis was superseded by a more conventional frame known as the 'MW' (medium weight). The basic
style of bodywork used for the MW was initially the same as the
last batch of LS coaches, ie 2203–14, except that a few new
features and improvements were incorporated. The heavy look-

BRISTOL/ECW 'MW' from 2270 onwards

Front elevation of MW coaches from No 2270 onwards

ing frontal apron was replaced by one with a radiator grill and passenger doors were installed which opened inwards. The first batch of Royal Blue MW coaches also saw the introduction of a brighter colour scheme insofar as these coaches were painted cream above waist level and over the roof. All subsequent deliveries of Royal Blue coaches have followed suit, and so the whole Royal Blue fleet, which hitherto had blue livery over the roof, was modified over a period of time.

In some respects the ECW style of coachwork was becoming outdated and in 1962 coach No 2270 was delivered with a restyled body design. The roof domes were unobstructed and the destination indicator was situated in the front apron, thereby departing from the Royal Blue indicator style which had been in use since 1935. The overall length of 31 ft took advantage of further revised 'Construction and Use Regulations' and with a seating capacity of 39, gave passengers more leg room.

All MW coaches from 1960 onwards have been delivered as 39-seaters. A further ten MW coaches of the new design, but fitted with air suspension, were delivered in 1963; No 2280 was, therefore, the last MW to be delivered for the Royal Blue fleet. This ended the 22xx class with which these coaches are identified. All have a Gardner 6HLW engine of 8.4 litre capacity mounted amidships, the engine being coupled with a standard Bristol 5-speed gearbox and friction clutch.

THE NEWEST COACHES

As a result of further revisions to the Construction and Use Regulations permitting construction of public service vehicles with 'box' dimensions not exceeding 36 ft x 8 ft $2\frac{1}{2}$ in, Bristol Commercial Vehicles developed the 'RE' series chassis which has the engine under the floor at the rear end. From the passenger's point of view noise level from the 10.45 litre Gardner engine has been reduced with the new position, as the sound tends to travel away from the vehicle as it moves forward.

Eastern Coach Works Limited designed the body in association with the chassis design carried out by Bristol Commercial

BRISTOL/ECW RELH6G 2351 onwards

Front elevation of RELH6G coach

Vehicles and so evolved the standard RE coach for the Tilling Group of Companies. Several new characteristics are featured in the body design, one being luggage space. Owing to the rear boot being reduced in size by the engine location, passenger's luggage is also carried in containers situated below floor level, to which access is gained by lifting the lower side panels. The heating system has been improved and the absence of opening windows forms part of the ventilation system in conjunction with jet-vents sited below the parcel shelf and individually controlled by each passenger.

The RE is regarded as an advanced vehicle offering improved safety, comfort, and good visibility and the first deliveries of this type to Royal Blue took place in 1964 when fourteen RELH6Gs were purchased. This and the second batch were fitted with friction clutches, but for the third batch and all subsequent deliveries semi-automatic transmission is standard. At the time of writing there are thirty-six RELH6G Royal Blue coaches in service and orders have been placed for several more to be delivered in 1970. The bodies follow the Tilling standard design, with small variations to fit them for use on regular express service work. All have front entrance/exit and seating for 45 persons.

APPENDIXES

APPENDIX A

SUMMARY OF PUBLIC SERVICE VEHICLES OPERATED UNDER THE 'ROYAL BLUE' FLEET NAME

1. As records no longer exist, details of horse-drawn vehicles, taxi, private hire or other cars have not been included.

2. Explanation of abbreviations, where used in accordance with information available:

   i. Ch—Char-a-banc.
   ii. DNK—Disposal not known.
   iii. C—Coach.
   iv. B—Bus.
   v. H & D—Hants & Dorset Motor Services Ltd.
   vi. WN—Western National Omnibus Company.
   vii. SN—Southern National Omnibus Company.
   viii. ?—Information not known.
   ix. Letter before fleet no.—Hants & Dorset numbering system.
   x. 'R' as suffix—rear passenger entrance.
   xi. 'F' as suffix—front passenger entrance.
   xii. *—denotes Southern National ownership; unstarred numbers are Western National vehicles.

3. Duple—'Duple Motor Bodies Limited'.

4. Beadle—'J. C. Beadle (Coachbuilders), Dartford'.

5. Eastern Counties—'Eastern Counties Omnibus Company Limited' (Lowestoft coach works).

6. ECW—'Eastern Coach Works Limited, Lowestoft'.

PART A: Vehicles owned by Elliott Bros and those which were subsequently transferred to Western National, Southern National, or Hants & Dorset

Fleet No	Regn No	Chassis		Body Make	Seats	Dates First Lic'd	Sold	Remarks
	EL1570	Dennis	28 hp	?	Ch20	20/ 3/13	18/ 1/15	Sold
	EL1571	Dennis	28 hp	?	Ch20	20/ 3/13	18/ 1/15	Sold
	EL1833	Daimler	40 hp	?	Ch26	3/ 7/13	?	DNK
	EL2000	Daimler	45 hp	?	Ch ?	3/ 4/14	29/ 5/15	Sold
	EL2001	,,	,,	?	Ch ?	1/ 7/14	1915/16	Sold to Admiralty (RNAS)

Fleet No	Regn No	Chassis		Body Make	Seats	First Lic'd	Sold	Remarks
	EL2200	Daimler	45 hp	?	Ch ?	25/ 7/14	?	DNK
	EL2300	,,	,,	?	Ch ?	4/ 8/14	17/ 8/14	Sold
	EL2625	Selden	35 hp	?	Ch ?	19/ 5/15	?	DNK
	EL2626	,,	,,	?	Ch ?	26/ 5/15	?	DNK
	EL2627	,,	,,	?	Ch ?	29/ 6/15	?	DNK
	EL2628	,,	,,	?	Ch ?	20/ 7/15	?	DNK
	EL2668	,,	,,	?	Ch ?	1/ 7/15	?	DNK
	EL2669	,,	,,	?	Ch ?	3/ 8/15	?	DNK
	EL1718	De Dion	25 hp	?	Ch ?	14/ 5/13	?	} ex W. Dinniven
	EL2038	De Dion	35 hp	?	Ch ?	7/ 4/14	?	} Westbourne 7/15
	EL3022	Selden	30/40 hp	?	Ch ?	22/ 4/16	?	DNK
	EL3023	,,	,,	?	Ch ?	17/ 4/16	?	DNK
	EL3024	,,	,,	?	Ch ?	22/ 4/16	?	DNK
	EL3070	,,	35 hp	?	Ch ?	12/ 6/16	?	DNK
	EL3071	,,	,,	?	Ch ?	12/ 6/16	?	DNK
	EL3118	,,	,,	?	Ch ?	24/ 7/16	?	DNK
	EL3119	,,	,,	?	Ch ?	24/ 7/16	?	DNK
	EL3120	,,	,,	?	Ch ?	24/ 7/16	?	DNK
	EL3121	,,	,,	?	Ch ?	24/ 7/16	?	Sold
	EL3602	AEC	YC	?	Ch ?	28/ 3/19	?	Sold
	EL3603	,,	,,	?	Ch ?	23/ 3/19	?	Sold
	EL3604	,,	,,	?	Ch26	27/ 3/19	?	Sold to AEC
	EL3605	,,	,,	?	Ch ?	25/ 3/19	?	Sold
	EL3606	,,	,,	?	Ch ?	7/ 4/19	?	Sold
	EL3607	,,	,,	?	Ch ?	7/ 4/19	?	Sold
	EL3731	Daimler	30 hp	?	Ch23	23/ 4/19	?	Sold
	EL3732	,,	,,	?	Ch14	23/ 4/19	9/28	DNK
	EL3733	,,	,,	?	Ch23	23/ 4/19	?	Sold
	EL3734	,,	,,	?	Ch20	23/ 4/19	?	Sold
	EL3735	,,	,,	?	Ch14	7/ 5/19	?	Sold
	EL3736	,,	,,	?	Ch14	7/ 5/19	?	Sold
	EL3737	,,	,,	Metcalf	Ch20	20/ 5/19	?	Sold
	EL3738	,,	,,	?	Ch ?	20/ 5/19	?	Sold
	EL3739	,,	,,	?	Ch23	20/ 5/19	9/26	Exported
	EL3740	,,	,,	?	Ch20	20/ 5/19	?	Sold
	EL3835	,,	,,	?	Ch ?	28/ 5/19	?	Sold
	EL3836	,,	,,	?	Ch ?	25/ 6/19	?	Sold
	EL3837	,,	,,	?	Ch ?	18/ 7/19	?	Sold
	EL3838	,,	,,	?	Ch ?	25/ 6/19	?	Sold
4B	EL3839	,,	,,	?	Ch ?	25/ 6/19	?	Sold
	EL3788	,,	,,	?	Ch29	1/ 7/19	?	} exBournemouth
	EL3789	,,	,,	?	Ch ?	2/ 7/19	?	} Motor Syndicate 28/10/19
	EL4943	Daimler	22 hp	?	Ch ?	14/ 6/20	6/27	Exported
	EL4944	,,	,,	?	Ch ?	14/ 6/20	6/27	Exported
	EL4945	,,	,,	?	Ch20	16/ 6/20	?	Sold
	EL4946	,,	,,	?	Ch ?	1/ 7/20	?	Exported
	EL4947	,,	,,	?	Ch ?	1/ 7/20	?	Sold
	EL5801	Daimler	30 hp	?	Ch26	24/12/20	?	Sold
	EL5857	Daimler	30 hp	?	Ch29	2/ 2/21	?	Sold
	EL5979	,,	,,	?	Ch28	23/ 5/21	?	Sold
	EL6188	,,	,,	?	Ch26	29/ 7/21	?	Sold
	EL6266	,,	,,	?	Ch ?	20/ 9/21	?	Sold
	EL6267	,,	,,	?	Ch ?	18/10/21	?	Sold
	EL6310	,,	,,	?	Ch ?	4/10/21	?	Sold
	EL6326	,,	,,	?	Ch ?	11/10/21	?	Sold
	EL3742	,,	,,	?	Ch ?	7/ 7/19	?	} exW & E Briant,
	EL3743	,,	,,	?	Ch ?	6/ 4/20	?	} Exeter Road,
	EL4976	,,	22 hp	?	Ch ?	26/ 5/20	?	} Bournemouth 1921
	EL6431	Daimler	Y	?	Ch ?	3/ 1/22	?	Exported
	EL6443	,,	,,	?	Ch ?	6/ 1/22	?	Sold
	EL6604	,,	,,	?	Ch ?	15/ 4/22	?	Sold
	EL6605	,,	,,	?	Ch26	14/ 4/22	?	Sold
	EL6791	,,	,,	?	Ch ?	16/ 8/22	?	Sold
	EL6902	,,	,,	?	Ch ?	3/ 6/22	?	Sold
	EL6903	,,	,,	?	Ch ?	3/ 6/22	?	Sold
	EL7169	,,	,,	?	Ch ?	10/10/22	?	Sold
	EL7245	,,	,,	?	Ch ?	20/11/22	?	Sold

Fleet No	Regn No	Chassis		Body Make	Seats	First Lic'd	Sold	Remarks
EL8771	Daimler	Y	Dodson	B 28	?		2/24	To H&D as 82
EL8772	,,	,,	,,	B 28	?		2/24	To H&D as 84
EL8773	,,	,,	,,	B 28	?		2/24	To H&D as 86
EL8900	,,	,,	,,	B 28	?		2/24	To H&D as 88
EL8901	,,	,,	,,	B 28	?		2/24	To H&D as 92
EL8902	,,	,,	,,	B 28	?		2/24	To H&D as 96
EL9188	,,	,,	,,	B 28	?		2/24	To H&D as 98
EL9385	,,	,,	,,	B 28	?		2/24	To H&D as 100
EL9410	,,	,,	,,	B 28	?		2/24	To H&D as 102
CR8636	,,	,,	,,	B 28	?		2/24	To H&D as 90
CR8828	,,	,,	,,	B 28	?		2/24	To H&D as 94
CR9081	,,	,,	,,	B 28	?		2/24	To H&D as 104
EL8795	Daimler	Y	?	Ch ?	4/ 2/24	?		Sold
EL8802	,,	,,	?	Ch ?	9/ 2/24	?		Sold
EL9635	,,	,,	?	Ch ?	11/ 7/24	?		Sold
EL9859	,,	,,	?	Ch ?	29/ 8/24	?		Sold
RU48	,,	,,	?	Ch ?	14/10/24	?		Sold
RU681	Daimler	Y	?	Ch ?	25/ 3/25	?		Sold
RU1182	,,	,,	?	Ch ?	23/ 5/25	?		Sold
RU1391	,,	,,	?	Ch ?	26/ 6/25	?		Sold
RU1440	,,	,,	?	Ch ?	27/ 6/25	?		Sold
EL8165	Crossley		?	Ch ?	13/ 7/23	?		)ex ? 1926
?	Daimler	Y	?	Ch ?	?	?		Believed to have
?	,,	,,	?	Ch ?	?	?		been bought
?	,,	,,	?	Ch ?	?	?		second - hand—
?	,,	CK	?	Ch ?	?	?		no further details known
RU6711	ADC	424	Hall Lewis	C 24	2/ 4/28	31/ 1/35		To WN as 3600
RU6712	,,	,,	,,	C 26	25/ 4/28	,,		To SN as 3700
RU6713	,,	,,	,,	C 26	25/ 4/28	,,		To H&D as N448
RU6714	,,	,,	Duple	C 23	5/ 4/28	,,		To WN as 3601
RU6715	,,	,,	,,	C 24	25/ 4/28	,,		To SN as 3701
RU6716	,,	,,	,,	C 26	25/ 4/28	,,		To H&D as N450
RU6717	,,	,,	,,	C 20	12/ 5/28	,,		To WN as 3602
RU6718	,,	,,	,,	C 23	17/ 5/28	,,		To SN as 3702
RU6719	,,	,,	,,	C 26	25/ 5/28	,,		To H&D as N452
RU6720	,,	,,	,,	C 24	25/ 5/28	,,		To WN as 3603
RU6721	,,	,,	,,	C 26	25/ 5/28	,,		To SN as 3703
RU6722	,,	,,	,,	C 26	26/ 5/28	,,		To H&D as N454
RU6723	,,	,,	,,	C 24	26/ 5/28	,,		To WN as 3604
RU6724	ADC	424	Hall Lewis	C 24	1/ 6/28	31/ 1/35		To SN as 3704
RU6725	,,	,,	,,	C 26	1/ 6/28	,,		To H&D as N456
RU6726	,,	,,	Duple	C 23	8/ 6/28	31/ 1/35		To WN as 3605
RU6727	,,	,,	,,	C 26	15/ 6/28	31/ 1/35		To SN as 3705
RU6728	,,	,,	,,	C 26	5/ 7/28	31/ 1/35		To H&D as N428
RU6729	,,	,,	,,	C 23	5/ 7/28	31/ 1/35		To WN as 3606
RU6730	,,	,,	,,	C 26	11/ 7/28	31/ 1/35		To SN as 3706
RU6731	,,	,,	,,	C 24	11/ 7/28	31/ 1/35		To H&D as N460
RU6732	,,	,,	,,	C 23	18/ 7/28	31/ 1/35		To WN as 3607
RU6733	,,	,,	,,	C 24	18/ 7/28	31/ 1/35		To SN as 3707
RU6734	,,	,,	,,	C 24	18/ 7/28	31/ 1/35		To H&D as N462
RU6735	,,	,,	,,	C 23	27/ 7/28	31/ 1/35		To WN as 3608
RU6736	,,	,,	,,	C 23	27/ 7/28	31/ 1/35		To SN as 3708
RU7730	ADC	426	Hall Lewis	C 28	25/ 7/28	31/ 1/35		To H&D
RU7731	,,	,,	,,	C 28	25/ 7/28	31/ 1/35		To WN as 3609
RU7732	,,	,,	,,	C 28	27/ 7/28	31/ 1/35		To WN as 3610
RU7733	,,	,,	,,	C 28	27/ 7/28	31/ 1/35		To SN as 3709
RU7734	,,	,,	,,	C 28	27/ 7/28	31/ 1/35		To H&D
RU7735	,,	,,	,,	C 28	27/ 7/28	31/ 1/35		To SN as 3710

These twelve vehicles were sold to Hants & Dorset Motor Services Ltd before entering service with Elliotts.

None of the vehicles that passed to Hants & Dorset from this batch were licensed by them. They were soon sold elsewhere. Western National 3600–3608 were sold to Willmott (dealer), Plymouth, in 1937. Southern National 3700/2/4/8 were sold to Dawson (breaker), Clapham in 1936, and 3701/3/5-7 passed to Talbot (dealer), Taunton, in August, 1937.

The ADC 426 chassis were reclassified AEC Reliance in November, 1929. Those vehicles which passed to Hants & Dorset were not numbered or operated by them and were sold elsewhere. Western National cars 3609/10 were rebodied by Beadle with 28-seater, rear entrance bodies in 1935. Car 3609 was sold to Lampo (breaker), Tedburn St Mary, and 3610 passed to Cumming (contractor), Burnham-on-Sea, both in 1950. Southern National cars 3709/10 received Beadle C28 bodies in 1936 and both were sold to Bowers (dealer), Chard, in December, 1949.

APPENDIXES

Fleet No	Regn No	Chassis		Body Make	Seats	First Lic'd	Sold	Remarks
RU8801	AEC	Reliance	Duple	C 28	25/ 3/29	31/ 1/35	To WN as 3611
RU8802	,,	,,	,,	C 28	25/ 3/29	31/ 1/35	To WN as 3612
RU8803	,,	,,	,,	C 28	25/ 3/29	31/ 1/35	To WN as 3613
RU8804	,,	,,	,,	C 28	25/ 3/29	31/ 1/35	To WN as 3614
RU8805	,,	,,	,,	C 28	25/ 3/29	31/ 1/35	To WN as 3615
RU8806	,,	,,	,,	C 28	25/ 3/29	31/ 1/35	To SN as 3711
RU8807	,,	,,	,,	C 28	11/ 4/29	31/ 1/35	To SN as 3712
RU8808	,,	,,	,,	C 28	11/ 4/29	31/ 1/35	To SN as 3713
RU8809	,,	,,	,,	C 32	15/ 4/29	31/ 1/35	To H&D
RU8810	,,	,,	,,	C 32	15/ 4/29	31/ 1/35	To SN as 3714
RU8811	,,	,,	,,	C 32	15/ 4/29	31/ 1/35	To WN as 3616
RU8812	,,	,,	,,	C 32	15/ 4/29	31/ 1/35	To SN as 3715
RU8813	AEC	Reliance	Duple	C 32	4/ 5/29	31/ 1/35	To SN as 3716
RU8814	,,	,,	,,	C 32	10/ 5/29	31/ 1/35	To H&D
RU8815	,,	,,	,,	C 32	10/ 5/29	31/ 1/35	To WN as 3617
RU8816	,,	,,	,,	C 28	14/ 5/29	31/ 1/35	To SN as 3717
RU8817	,,	,,	,,	C 28	14/ 5/29	31/ 1/35	To H&D
RU8818	,,	,,	,,	C 28	3/ 6/29	31/ 1/35	To WN as 3618
RU8819	,,	,,	,,	C 28	3/ 6/29	31/ 1/35	To SN as 3718
RU8820	,,	,,	,,	C 28	3/ 6/29	31/ 1/35	To H&D
RU8821	,,	,,	,,	C 28	3/ 6/29	31/ 1/35	To H&D
RU8822	,,	,,	,,	C 28	3/ 6/29	31/ 1/35	To H&D
RU8823	,,	,,	,,	C 28	3/ 6/29	31/ 1/35	To H&D
RU8824	,,	,,	,,	C 28	3/ 6/29	31/ 1/35	To H&D
RU8825	,,	,,	,,	C 30	3/ 6/29	31/ 1/35	To H&D
RU9030	Daimler	CF6	Duple	C 30	19/ 6/29	31/ 1/35	To H&D as N414
RU9031	,,	,,	,,	C 32	19/ 6/29	31/ 1/35	To WN as 3619
RU9032	,,	,,	,,	C 32	19/ 6/29	31/ 1/35	To WN as 3620
RU9033	,,	,,	,,	C 28	19/ 6/29	31/ 1/35	To SN as 3719
RU9034	,,	,,	,,	C 28	19/ 6/29	31/ 1/35	To SN as 3720
RU9035	,,	,,	,,	C 28	19/ 6/29	31/ 1/35	To H&D as N416
LJ650	AEC	Regal	Duple	C 31	30/11/29	31/ 1/35	To SN as 3721
LJ651	Maudslay	ML6	,,	C 31	30/11/29	31/ 1/35	To WN as 3621
LJ652	Daimler	CF6	,,	C 28	30/11/29	31/ 1/35	To WN as 3622
LJ875	Leyland	TS2	,,	C 28	28/ 2/30	31/ 1/35	To H&D as F412
LJ1501	Daimler	CF6	Duple	C 28	3/ 6/30	31/ 1/35	To H&D as N418
LJ1502	,,	,,	,,	C 28	3/ 6/30	31/ 1/35	To SN as 3722
LJ1503	,,	,,	,,	C 28	3/ 6/30	31/ 1/35	To SN as 3723
LJ1504	,,	,,	,,	C 30	3/ 6/30	31/ 1/35	To H&D as N420
LJ1505	,,	,,	,,	C 28	3/ 6/30	31/ 1/35	To SN as 3724
LJ1506	,,	,,	,,	C 28	3/ 6/30	31/ 1/35	To WN as 3623
LJ1507	,,	,,	,,	C 32	26/ 6/30	31/ 1/35	To H&D as N422
LJ1508	,,	,,	,,	C 32	26/ 6/30	31/ 1/30	To WN as 3624
LJ1509	,,	,,	,,	C 28	26/ 6/30	31/ 1/35	To SN as 3725
LJ1510	AEC	Regal	Duple	C 31	3/ 6/30	31/ 1/35	To WN as 3626
LJ1511	,,	,,	,,	C 31	19/ 6/30	31/ 1/35	To WN as 3627
LJ1512	,,	,,	,,	C 33	19/ 6/30	31/ 1/35	To SN as 3728
LJ1513	,,	,,	,,	C 32	19/ 6/30	31/ 1/35	To WN as 3628
LJ1514	,,	,,	,,	C 32	3/ 6/30	31/ 1/35	To WN as 3629
LJ1515	,,	,,	,,	C 32	19/ 6/30	31/ 1/35	To WN as 3630
LJ1516	,,	,,	,,	C 28	3/ 7/30	31/ 1/35	To H&D as J428
LJ1517	,,	,,	,,	C 31	3/ 7/30	31/ 1/35	To H&D as J430
LJ1518	,,	,,	,,	C 31	3/ 7/30	31/ 1/35	To H&D as J432
LJ1519	,,	,,	,,	C 32	3/ 7/30	31/ 1/35	To W&N as 3631
LJ1520	,,	,,	,,	C 28	3/ 7/30	31/ 1/35	To H&D as J434
LJ1521	,,	,,	,,	C 32	3/ 7/30	31/ 1/35	To WN as 3632
LJ1522	,,	,,	,,	C 31	3/ 6/30	31/ 1/35	To SN as 3729
LJ1523	,,	,,	,,	C 28	3/ 6/30	31/ 1/35	To H&D as J436
LJ1524	,,	,,	,,	C 31	3/ 6/30	31/ 1/35	To SN as 3730
LJ1525	,,	,,	,,	C 31	3/ 6/30	31/ 1/35	To SN as 3731
LJ1526	,,	,,	,,	C 31	19/ 6/30	31/ 1/35	To H&D as J438
LJ1527	,,	,,	,,	C 32	19/ 6/30	31/ 1/35	To SN as 3732

Those vehicles in this batch which passed to Hants & Dorset were not numbered or operated by them and were sold elsewhere. Western National cars 3612/16/17/18 were sold in 1937. Cars 3611/13/14/15 received Beadle C28 bodies in 1935-6 and were sold 1950, 1951, 1949, and 1950 respectively. Southern National cars 3713/14/15/16/18 were sold in 1937. Cars 3711/12/17 received Beadle C28 bodies in 1936 and were sold in 1948, 1948, and 1949 respectively.

The two vehicles from this batch which passed to Hants & Dorset were used by them for a while before being sold elsewhere. The vehicles which passed to Western and Southern National were all broken up after a short spell of service. Cars 3619/20 in 1938 and 3719/20 in 1937.

Cars 3621 and 3622 were used for a while by Western National before being sold in December, 1937 Southern National car 3721 received a Beadle C31 body in 1937 and was transferred to the Southern National coach fleet. It was eventually sold in March, 1954. This coach in its original form appeared at the 1929 Commercial Motor Show. The coach which became Hants & Dorset F412 was operated by them.

Those vehicles which passed to Hants & Dorset were used by them. Western National cars 3623/4 were broken up in January, 1938 after a period of service. Southern National cars 3722/5 were sold to North (dealer), Leeds, in December, 1937, after a period of service.

Those vehicles which passed to Hants & Dorset were used by them. Western National car 3626 received a Beadle C31 body in 1937 and was broken up by the company in March, 1954. Car 3627 received a Beadle C32 body in 1936 and was sold to Thompson (dealer) Cardiff, in October 1953. Car 3631 received a Beadle C32 body in 1939. This vehicle was severely damaged by enemy action in August 1943 and was broken up by the company early in 1944. Car 3632 received a Duple C32 body in 1936 and was transferred to the Western National coach fleet. Cars 3628/9/30 received Duple C32 bodies in 1938. These vehicles were sold in 1952, 1953, and 1952 respectively and car 3632 was sold in October, 1953. Southern National cars were rebodied as follows :

3728 Duple C33 1938	3731 Beadle C32 1936
3729 Beadle C31 1937	3732 Duple C32 1938 and transferred to
3730 Beadle C32 1936	the Southern National fleet.

3730 again in August, 1949 with the original body from car 1050.
3732 was damaged by enemy action October, 1940 but after repairs continued in service.

Disposals
3728 broken up by Southern National November, 1953
3729 and 3731 broken up by Southern National March, 1954
3730 broken up by Southern National March, 1954
3732 Thompson (dealer), Cardiff, October, 1953

M

Fleet No	Regn No	Chassis		Body Make	Seats	First Lic'd	Sold	Remarks
	TP9181	Gilford	1680T	Weymann	C 26	?/ ?/30	31/ 1/35	To H&D as 410
	TP9182	,,	,,	,,	C 26	?/ ?/30	31/ 1/35	To WN as 3635
	TP9329	Chevrolet	,,	Reading	C 14	?/ 7/30	31/ 1/35	To SN as 3733
	TP9360	,,		,,	C 14	?/ 7/30	31/ 1/35	To WN as 3634
	PJ5494	Dennis	Lancet	Dennis	C 26	?/ 5/32	31/ 1/35	To WN as 3633
	??8656	Gilford		?	C 30	?/ ?/29	31/ 1/35	To SN as 3734
	LJ8001	AEC	'Q'	Duple	C 35	?/ 8/33	31/ 1/35	To H&D as Q444
	LJ8600	,,	,,	,,	C 35	30/11/33	31/ 1/35	To H&D as Q440
	LJ8601	,,	,,	,,	C 37	28/ 3/34	31/ 1/35	To H&D as Q442
	AEL2	,,	,,	Harrington	C 35	1/ 6/34	31/ 1/35	To H&D as Q446
	AEL495	Leyland	,,	?	C ?	6/ 7/34	31/ 1/35	To H&D

PART B: Vehicles purchased by Western/Southern National Omnibus Companies from 1935 which have been operated in the Royal Blue fleet in addition to those transferred by purchase of Elliott Bros (Bournemouth) Ltd.

Fleet No	Regn No	Chassis		Body Make	Seats	First Lic'd	Sold
163	BTA453	Bristol	JJW	ECOC	C32R	3/35	11/58
*164	BTA454	,,	,,	,,	,,	3/35	12/58
165	BTA455	,,	,,	,,	,,	3/35	10/58
*166	BTA456	,,	,,	,,	,,	3/35	12/58
167	BTA457	,,	,,	,,	,,	3/35	10/58
*168	BTA458	,,	,,	,,	,,	3/35	9/58
169	BTA459	,,	,,	,,	,,	3/35	11/58
*170	BTA460	,,	,,	,,	,,	3/35	9/58
171	ATT921	,,	,,	Beadle	,,	8/35	10/58
172	ATT922	,,	,,	,,	,,	8/35	11/58
173	ATT923	,,	,,	,,	,,	8/35	10/58
174	ATT924	,,	,,	,,	,,	8/35	12/58
175	ATT925	,,	,,	MCW	,,	8/35	12/58
176	ATT926	,,	,,	,,	,,	8/35	12/58
177	ATT927	,,	,,	,,	,,	8/35	11/58
178	ATT928	,,	,,	Beadle	,,	8/35	12/58
179	ATT929	,,	,,	MCW	,,	8/35	12/58
180	ATT930	,,	,,	,,	,,	9/35	10/58
*181	ATT931	,,	,,	Beadle	,,	7/35	9/58
*182	ATT932	,,	,,	MCW	,,	8/35	9/58
*183	ATT933	,,	,,	,,	,,	8/35	10/58
*184	ATT934	,,	,,	Beadle	,,	7/35	10/58
*185	ATT935	,,	,,	,,	,,	7/35	12/58
*186	ATT936	,,	,,	MCW	,,	8/35	12/58
*187	ATT937	,,	,,	,,	,,	8/35	11/58
*188	ATT938	,,	,,	,,	,,	8/35	10/58
*189	ATT939	,,	,,	Beadle	,,	7/35	11/58
*190	ATT940	,,	,,	,,	,,	7/35	10/58

* SN vehicles. WN unstarred.

The vehicles opposite were acquired from Traveller Coaches, Portsmouth, July 1932.

The last Gilford vehicle listed has been claimed to be registered UV8656 but this does not correspond with Greater London Council taxation records. The two 'TP' registered Gilford machines were originally in the fleet of Olympic Motor Services, Southsea.

DISPOSALS

The Gilford which passed to Hants & Dorset was sold almost immediately. The Dennis Lancet was completely destroyed by enemy action at Plymouth, March 1941. This vehicle had been transferred to the Western National coach fleet in 1937. Car 3634 was sold almost immediately to Blundell, Christchurch. Car 3635 operated as a Southern National coach for one season and was sold to Dawson (breaker), Clapham in September, 1936. Southern National car 3733 was sold in November, 1935 and never operated as a Royal Blue vehicle whilst with Southern National. The Gilford 3734 was used as a Southern National coach until September, 1936 when it was sold to Dawson (breaker), Clapham.

The Leyland coach is something of a mystery; Hants & Dorset have no record of it and the taxation records indicate that it was last licensed in January 1947 as a lorry with Maidment, Preston. The four AEC 'Q's each saw several more years service with Hants & Dorset.

Vehicle 167 was delivered as a Western National coach and did not enter the Royal Blue fleet until August, 1937. The same applies to vehicles 184 and 188 which arrived new as Southern National coaches. Vehicles 163–70, 173–4, 177–9, 184, 186–8 and 190 all operated on producer gas during the War. Vehicle 164 was delivered new in a modified livery which incorporated cream beading. This was not adopted generally and subsequently 164 was repainted in the standard livery. Between 1946 and 1949, the batch of coaches was downgraded and bus bodies were fitted by John Beadle.

Fleet No	Regn No	Chassis		Body Make	Seats	Dates First Lic'd	Sold
3568	DV4890	Leyland	TS2	Beadle	C32	4/30	10/53
3569	DV4891	,,	,,	,,	,,	4/30	1/53
3570	DV4889	,,	,,	,,	,,	4/30	1/53
3571	DV4925	,,	,,	,,	,,	4/30	10/53
3572	DV5475	,,	,,	,,	,,	5/30	1/53
3573	DV5476	,,	,,	,,	,,	5/30	10/53
*3574	DV5477	,,	TS3	,,	C28	5/30	6/50
*3575	DV5478	,,	,,	,,	,,	5/30	9/52
*3576	DV5479	,,	,,	,,	,,	5/30	6/52
*3577	DV5480	,,	,,	,,	,,	5/30	9/52
1050	ETA976	AEC	Regal	Mumford	C31	10/37	4/57
1051	ETA977	,,	,,	,,	,,	10/37	4/57
1052	ETA978	,,	,,	,,	,,	10/37	4/57
1053	ETA979	,,	,,	,,	,,	11/37	4/57
1054	ETA980	,,	,,	,,	,,	11/37	4/57
1055	ETA981	,,	,,	,,	,,	10/37	4/57
1056	ETA982	,,	,,	,,	,,	12/37	4/57
1057	ETA983	,,	,,	,,	,,	12/37	4/57
*1058	ETA992	,,	,,	Duple	,,	7/37	4/57
*1059	ETA993	,,	,,	,,	,,	7/37	4/57
*1060	ETA994	,,	,,	,,	,,	7/37	4/57
*1061	ETA995	,,	,,	,,	,,	7/37	4/57
*1062	ETA996	,,	,,	,,	,,	7/37	4/57
*1063	ETA997	,,	,,	,,	,,	7/37	4/57
*1064	ETA998	,,	,,	,,	,,	7/37	4/57
*1065	ETA999	,,	,,	,,	,,	7/37	4/57
2863	UU1566	Leyland	TS2	Beadle	C26	5/29	1/53
2864	DR5255	,,	,,	,,	,,	5/29	10/53
2866	UU1567	,,	,,	,,	,,	5/29	1/53
*2981	DR6955	,,	TS3	,,	C28	4/30	9/52
*2982	DR6956	,,	,,	,,	,,	4/30	9/52
3527	TR9516	,,	,,	,,	,,	11/30	1/53
*2794	UU1565	Leyland	TS1	Beadle	C31	5/29	1/53
3140	DR8638	Leyland	TS1	Beadle	C31	5/31	1/53
3141	DR8806	,,	,,	,,	,,	6/31	1/53
3142	DR8882	,,	,,	,,	,,	6/31	1/53
*3104	YD2307	,,	,,	,,	,,	5/31	9/52
*3105	TK6402	,,	,,	,,	,,	5/31	1/53
*3537	TR9922	,,	,,	,,	,,	3/31	3/54
*3540	OW3167	AEC	Regal	Duple	,,	6/33	8/55
1200	JUO932	Bristol	L6B	Beadle	C31	5/48	
1201	JUO933	,,	,,	,,	,,	5/48	
1202	JUO934	,,	,,	,,	,,	6/48	
1203	JUO935	,,	,,	,,	,,	6/48	
1204	JUO936	,,	,,	,,	,,	6/48	
1205	JUO937	,,	,,	,,	,,	7/48	
1206	JUO938	,,	,,	,,	,,	7/48	
1207	JUO939	,,	,,	,,	,,	7/48	
1208	JUO940	,,	,,	,,	,,	7/48	
1209	JUO941	,,	,,	,,	,,	8/48	
1210	JUO942	,,	,,	,,	,,	8/48	
1211	JUO943	,,	,,	,,	,,	8/48	
1212	JUO944	,,	,,	,,	,,	8/48	
*1213	JUO978	,,	,,	,,	,,	8/48	
*1214	JUO979	,,	,,	,,	,,	8/48	
*1215	JUO980	,,	,,	,,	,,	8/48	
*1216	JUO981	,,	,,	,,	,,	8/48	
*1217	JUO982	,,	,,	,,	,,	8/48	
*1218	JUO983	,,	,,	,,	,,	8/48	
*1219	JUO984	,,	,,	,,	,,	9/48	
*1220	JUO985	,,	,,	,,	,,	9/48	
*1221	JUO986	,,	,,	,,	,,	9/48	
*1222	JUO987	,,	,,	,,	,,	9/48	
*1223	JUO988	,,	,,	,,	,,	9/48	
*1224	JUO989	,,	,,	,,	,,	9/48	
1225	HOD27	,,	L6A	,,	,,	9/48	
1226	HOD28	,,	,,	,,	,,	9/48	4/60
1227	HOD29	,,	,,	,,	,,	9/48	4/60

The ten vehicles opposite were acquired from Devon General Omnibus & Touring Company in October 1935 and were rebodied by Beadle before entering the Royal Blue fleet in 1936. Vehicles 3568–73 operated on producer gas during the War. They were also hired to the military authorities for troop carrying duties.

This batch of vehicles remained in the Royal Blue fleet throughout the twenty years with Western and Southern National. They were all rebodied with front entrance Beadle bodies in 1949 except vehicle 1062 which, having caught fire at Tidworth in 1939, received a Duple body soon after.

Vehicles 2863–4 and 2866 were three existing Western National coaches rebodied by Beadle in 1937 for the Royal Blue fleet. Vehicles 2981–2 were two Southern National coaches rebodied in 1937 by Beadle for the Royal Blue fleet. Vehicle 3527 was acquired from Tourist Motor Coaches, Southampton in May, 1935 and was rebodied by Beadle in 1937 for the Royal Blue fleet.

Vehicle 2794 was an existing Southern National coach rebodied by Beadle in 1938 for the Royal Blue fleet.

Vehicles 3140–42 were existing Western National coaches rebodied by Beadle in 1939 for the Royal Blue fleet. Vehicles 3104–5 were existing Southern National coaches rebodied by Beadle in 1939 for the Royal Blue fleet. Vehicles 3537 and 3540 were acquired from Tourist Motor Coaches, Southampton, in May 1935, and were rebodied by Beadle and Duple respectively in 1939 for the Royal Blue fleet.

In 1958, the coach bodies on vehicles 1200–25 inclusive were removed and scrapped or sold and the chassis were completely stripped. New frame sections were obtained from Bristol and the chassis were rebuilt at Plymouth incorporating latest modifications and rear frame extensions. The chassis were then reclassified as 'LL' and were sent to Lowestoft for fitment of OMB bus bodies by Eastern Coach Works. In every case, the registration numbers, chassis numbers, and fleet numbers all remained the same and the entire batch are still with Western/Southern National.

Vehicles 1226–8, 1235, and 1237 were all sold to a dealer in April, 1960. Vehicle 1236 was severely damaged by fire at Marlborough in 1954 and was later rebodied as a bus by Bristol Tramways & Carriage Co Ltd on a lengthened chassis. This vehicle was sold to a dealer in December, 1966.

Fleet No	Regn No	Chassis		Body Make	Seats	First Lic'd	Sold
1228	HOD30	Bristol	L6A	Beadle	C31	10/48	4/60
*1235	HOD98	,,	,,	,,	,,	9/48	4/60
*1236	HOD99	,,	,,	,,	,,	10/48	12/66
*1237	HOD100	,,	,,	,,	,,	10/48	4/60
1229	HOD31	,,		,,	,,	2/49	4/60
1230	HOD365	,,	L6B	,,	,,	8/49	3/60
1231	HOD33	,,	,,	,,	,,	8/49	3/60
1232	HOD34	,,	,,	,,	,,	8/49	10/61
1233	HOD35	,,	,,	,,	,,	10/49	10/61
1234	HOD36	,,	,,	,,	,,	10/49	9/61
*1238	HOD101	,,	L6A	,,	,,	2/49	4/60
*1239	HOD102	,,	,,	,,	,,	3/49	4/60
*1240	HOD103	,,	L6B	,,	,,	8/49	4/60
*1241	HOD104	,,	,,	,,	,,	9/49	4/60
*1242	HOD105	,,	,,	,,	,,	10/49	9/61
*1243	HOD106	,,	,,	,,	,,	10/49	9/61
*1244	HOD107	,,	,,	,,	,,	10/49	9/61
1245	LTA724	,,	,,	Duple	C33	9/50	10/61
1246	LTA725	,,	,,	,,	,,	9/50	9/62
1247	LTA726	,,	,,	,,	,,	9/50	10/61
1248	LTA727	,,	,,	,,	,,	9/50	11/61
1249	LTA728	,,	,,	,,	,,	9/50	11/61
*1259	LTA888	,,	,,	,,	,,	8/50	10/61
*1260	LTA889	,,	,,	,,	,,	8/50	10/61
*1261	LTA890	,,	,,	,,	,,	8/50	6/61
*1262	LTA891	,,	,,	,,	,,	8/50	10/61
*1263	LTA892	,,	,,	,,	,,	9/50	10/61
1250	LTA729	Bristol	LL6B	Duple	C37	3/51	1/64
1251	LTA730	,,	,,	,,	,,	3/51	2/64
1252	LTA731	,,	,,	,,	,,	3/51	2/64
1253	LTA732	,,	,,	,,	,,	3/51	2/64
1254	LTA733	,,	,,	,,	,,	3/51	2/64
1255	LTA734	,,	,,	,,	,,	3/51	4/64
1256	LTA735	,,	,,	,,	,,	5/51	2/64
1257	LTA736	,,	,,	,,	,,	5/51	2/65
1258	LTA737	,,	,,	,,	,,	5/51	2/64
*1264	LTA893	Bristol	LL6B	Duple	C37	3/51	2/64
*1265	LTA894	,,	,,	,,	,,	3/51	2/65
*1266	LTA895	,,	,,	,,	,,	3/51	3/63
*1267	LTA896	,,	,,	,,	,,	3/51	2/64
*1268	LTA897	,,	,,	,,	,,	5/51	2/64
*1269	LTA898	,,	,,	,,	,,	5/51	1/64
*1270	LTA899	,,	,,	,,	,,	5/51	2/65
*1271	LTA900	,,	,,	,,	,,	5/51	3/64
*1272	LTA966	,,	,,	,,	,,	5/51	2/64
*1273	LTA967	,,	,,	,,	,,	5/51	2/64
*1274	LTA968	,,	,,	,,	,,	5/51	2/64
*1275	LTA969	,,	,,	,,	,,	5/51	2/64
1276	LTA864	,,	,,	,,	,,	5/51	1/64
1277	LTA865	,,	,,	,,	,,	5/51	1/64
1278	LTA866	,,	,,	,,	,,	5/51	2/64
1279	LTA867	Bristol	LS6G	ECW	C41	7/52	4/67
1280	LTA868	,,	,,	,,	,,	7/52	4/67
1281	LTA869	,,	,,	,,	,,	7/52	7/68
1282	LTA870	,,	,,	,,	,,	7/52	4/67
1283	LTA871	,,	,,	,,	,,	8/52	7/68
1284	LTA872	,,	,,	,,	,,	9/52	7/68
1285	LTA873	,,	,,	,,	,,	10/52	4/67
*1286	MOD973	,,	,,	,,	,,	9/52	7/68
*1287	MOD974	,,	,,	,,	,,	8/52	4/67
*1288	MOD975	,,	,,	,,	,,	7/52	4/67
*1289	MOD976	,,	,,	,,	,,	8/52	7/68
*1290	MOD977	,,	,,	,,	,,	9/52	7/68
*1291	MOD978	,,	,,	,,	,,	9/52	7/68
*1292	MOD979	,,	,,	,,	,,	10/52	7/68
*1293	OTT92	Bristol	LS6G	ECW	C41	8/53	
*1294	OTT93	,,	,,	,,	,,	9/53	6/69
*1295	OTT94	,,	,,	,,	,,	8/53	5/69
*1296	OTT95	,,	,,	,,	,,	9/53	4/69
*1297	OTT96	,,	,,	,,	,,	8/53	**
*1298	OTT97	,,	,,	,,	,,	9/53	4/69
*1299	OTT98	,,	,,	,,	,,	9/53	**

Vehicle 1246 was used as a public waiting room at Bridgwater bus station site between July, 1961 and July, 1962.

During the early part of 1960, vehicles 1279–92 were reupholstered at Eastern Coach Works, Lowestoft. The seating capacity was reduced to 39 at the same time. Vehicle 1286 was transferred from Southern to Western National in March 1962.

This batch of vehicles was reupholstered by Eastern Coach Works, Lowestoft, as follows: 1293–6 December 1960; 1297–8 January 1961; 1299, 2200–02 October 1961. The seating capacity was reduced to 39 at the same time.

** Held for disposal 9/69

Fleet No	Regn No	Chassis		Body Make	Seats	Dates First Lic'd	Sold
2200	OTT43	Bristol	LS6G	ECW	C41	8/53	5/69
2201	OTT44	,,	,,	,,	,,	8/53	5/69
2202	OTT45	,,	,,	,,	,,	9/53	
2203	VDV746	Bristol	LS6G	ECW	C41	2/57	
2204	VDV747	,,	,,	,,	,,	3/57	
2205	VDV748	,,	,,	,,	,,	3/57	
2206	VDV749	,,	,,	,,	,,	3/57	
2207	VDV750	,,	,,	,,	,,	4/57	
2208	VDV751	,,	,,	,,	,,	4/57	
*2209	VDV772	,,	,,	,,	,,	4/57	
*2210	VDV773	,,	,,	,,	,,	4/57	
*2211	VDV774	,,	,,	,,	,,	4/57	
*2212	VDV775	,,	,,	,,	,,	4/57	
*2213	VDV776	,,	,,	,,	,,	4/57	
*2214	VDV777	,,	,,	,,	,,	5/57	
*2215	XUO725	Bristol	MW6G	ECW	C41	3/58	
*2216	XUO726	,,	,,	,,	,,	5/58	
*2217	XUO727	,,	,,	,,	,,	3/58	
*2218	XUO728	,,	,,	,,	,,	5/58	
*2219	XUO729	,,	,,	,,	,,	5/58	
*2220	XUO730	,,	,,	,,	,,	5/58	
*2221	XUO731	,,	,,	,,	,,	5/58	
*2222	XUO732	,,	,,	,,	,,	6/58	
*2223	XUO733	,,	,,	,,	,,	6/58	
*2224	XUO734	,,	,,	,,	,,	6/58	
*2225	XUO735	,,	,,	,,	,,	6/58	
*2226	XUO736	,,	,,	,,	,,	6/58	
*2227	XUO737	,,	,,	,,	,,	7/58	
2228	XUO711	,,	,,	,,	,,	3/58	
2229	XUO712	,,	,,	,,	,,	3/58	
2230	XUO713	,,	,,	,,	,,	3/58	
2231	XUO714	,,	,,	,,	,,	3/58	
2232	XUO715	,,	,,	,,	,,	3/58	
2233	XUO716	,,	,,	,,	,,	3/58	
2234	XUO717	,,	,,	,,	,,	5/58	
2235	XUO718	,,	,,	,,	,,	5/58	
2236	XUO719	,,	,,	,,	,,	5/58	
2237	XUO720	,,	,,	,,	,,	5/58	
2238	XUO721	,,	,,	,,	,,	6/58	
2239	XUO722	,,	,,	,,	,,	6/58	
2240	XUO723	,,	,,	,,	,,	6/58	
2241	XUO724	,,	,,	,,	,,	7/58	
2242	621DDV	Bristol	MW6G	ECW	C39	3/60	
2243	622DDV	,,	,,	,,	,,	4/60	
2244	623DDV	,,	,,	,,	,,	3/60	
2245	624DDV	,,	,,	,,	,,	4/60	
2246	625DDV	,,	,,	,,	,,	5/60	
2247	626DDV	,,	,,	,,	,,	5/60	
*2248	615DDV	,,	,,	,,	,,	6/60	
*2249	616DDV	,,	,,	,,	,,	6/60	
*2250	617DDV	,,	,,	,,	,,	6/60	
*2251	618DDV	,,	,,	,,	,,	6/60	
*2252	619DDV	,,	,,	,,	,,	6/60	
*2253	620DDV	,,	,,	,,	,,	6/60	
*2254	59GUO	Bristol	MW6G	ECW	C39	6/61	
*2255	60GUO	,,	,,	,,	,,	6/61	
*2256	61GUO	,,	,,	,,	,,	6/61	
*2257	62GUO	,,	,,	,,	,,	6/61	
*2258	63GUO	,,	,,	,,	,,	6/61	
*2259	64GUO	,,	,,	,,	,,	6/61	
*2260	65GUO	,,	,,	,,	,,	6/61	
*2261	66GUO	,,	,,	,,	,,	6/61	
2262	51GUO	,,	,,	,,	,,	6/61	
2263	52GUO	,,	,,	,,	,,	6/61	
2264	53GUO	,,	,,	,,	,,	6/61	
2265	54GUO	,,	,,	,,	,,	6/61	
2266	55GUO	,,	,,	,,	,,	6/61	
2267	56GUO	,,	,,	,,	,,	6/61	
2268	57GUO	,,	,,	,,	,,	6/61	
2269	58GUO	,,	,,	,,	,,	6/61	

This batch of vehicles was reupholstered by Eastern Coach Works, Lowestoft, as follows: 2203/4/7, 2214 December 1964; 2212/13 January 1965; 2205/6/10 February 1965; 2208–11 March 1965; 2209 April 1965. The seating capacity was reduced to 39 at the same time.

This batch of vehicles was reduced to 39-seaters as follows:

C39	Plymouth	3/67
,,	,,	5/67
,,	,,	12/66
,,	,,	12/66
,,	,,	12/66
,,	,,	1/67
,,	,,	11/66
,,	,,	2/66
,,	,,	9/66
,,	,,	10/66
,,	,,	3/66
,,	,,	6/66
,,	,,	4/67
,,	,,	7/66
,,	,,	1/67
,,	,,	5/66
,,	,,	3/66
,,	,,	2/67
,,	,,	3/67
,,	,,	1/66
,,	,,	2/67
,,	,,	12/65
,,	,,	4/66
,,	,,	2/67
,,	,,	3/67
,,	,,	4/66
,,	,,	4/66

Fleet No	Regn No	Chassis		Body Make	Seats	Dates First Lic'd	Sold
2270	253KTA	Bristol	MW6G	ECW	C39	4/62	
2271	746MDV	"	"	"	"	6/63	
2272	747MDV	"	"	"	"	6/63	
*2273	761MDV	"	"	"	"	4/63	
*2274	762MDV	"	"	"	"	4/63	
*2275	763MDV	"	"	"	"	4/63	
*2276	764MDV	"	"	"	"	5/63	
*2277	765MDV	"	"	"	"	5/63	
*2278	766MDV	"	"	"	"	5/63	
*2279	767MDV	"	"	"	"	5/63	
*2280	768MDV	"	"	"	"	5/63	
2351	837SUO	Bristol	RELH6G	ECW	C45	5/64	
2352	838SUO	"	"	"	"	6/64	
2353	839SUO	"	"	"	"	6/64	
2354	840SUO	"	"	"	"	6/64	
2355	393TUO	"	"	"	"	6/64	
2356	394TUO	"	"	"	"	6/64	
2357	ATA101B	"	"	"	"	7/64	
2358	ATA102B	"	"	"	"	7/64	
2359	ATA103B	"	"	"	"	7/64	
2360	ATA104B	"	"	"	"	7/64	
*2361	841SUO	"	"	"	"	6/64	
*2362	842SUO	"	"	"	"	6/64	
*2363	ATA105B	"	"	"	"	7/64	
*2364	ATA106B	"	"	"	"	7/64	
*2365	HDV624E	Bristol	RELH6G	ECW	C45	3/67	
*2366	HDV625E	"	"	"	"	3/67	
2367	HDV642E	"	"	"	"	3/67	
2368	HDV643E	"	"	"	"	3/67	
2369	HDV644E	"	"	"	"	3/67	
2370	HDV645E	"	"	"	"	3/67	
2371	LDV843F	Bristol	RELH6G	ECW	C45	5/68	
2372	LDV844F	"	"	"	"	6/68	
2373	LDV845F	"	"	"	"	6/68	
2374	LDV846F	"	"	"	"	6/68	
*2375	LDV847F	"	"	"	"	3/68	
*2376	LDV848F	"	"	"	"	4/68	
*2377	LDV849F	"	"	"	"	5/68	
*2378	LDV850F	"	"	"	"	5/68	
*2379	OTA639G	Bristol	RELH6G	ECW	C45	3/69	
*2380	OTA640G	"	"	"	"	3/69	
*2381	OTA641G	"	"	"	"	3/69	
*2382	OTA642G	"	"	"	"	3/69	
2383	OTA643G	"	"	"	"	3/69	
2384	OTA644G	"	"	"	"	3/69	
2385	OTA645G	"	"	"	"	3/69	
2386	OTA646G	"	"	"	"	3/69	

This batch of vehicles is fitted with air suspension

This batch of vehicles is fitted with air suspension

This batch of vehicles has air suspension with leaf spring stabilisers

This batch of vehicles has leaf spring suspension and semi-automatic transmission

This batch of vehicles has leaf spring suspension and semi-automatic transmission with lock-up clutch

APPENDIX B

SUMMARY OF ROYAL BLUE FLEET STRENGTH FROM 1935 ON

Year	Intake	Disposal	Annual Balance	Fleet Strength
1935	*71* + 25 = 96	*4*	92	92
1936	*10*	*4*	6	98
1937	*6* + 19 = 25	*36*	−11	87
1938	*1*	*4*	− 3	84
1939	*7*	0	7	91
1941	0	0	0	91
1944	0	*1*	− 1	90
1947	0	10	−10	80
1948	32	2 + *2* = 4	28	108
1949	13	*4* + 16 = 20	− 7	101
1950	10	*5*	5	106
1951	24	*1*	23	129
1952	14	8	6	135
1953	10	*20*	−10	125
1954	0	5 + *1* = 6	− 6	119
1955	0	*1*	− 1	118
1957	12	16	− 4	114
1958	27	26	1	115
1960	12	11	1	116
1961	16	16	0	116
1962	1	1	0	116
1963	10	1	9	125
1964	14	20	− 6	119
1965	0	3	− 3	116
1967	6	6	0	116
1968	8	8	0	116
1969	8	8	0	116
TOTALS	356	240	116	116

NOTE: Italic figures denote the 95 secondhand or rehabilitated vehicles in the fleet.

It is interesting to observe that the last Elliott Royal Blue coach to be withdrawn was LJ 1525, a 1930 AEC Regal with 1936 Beadle body on 17.3.54. The first new Royal Blue coaches bought by Western and Southern National were replaced some 7 years earlier in 1947.

APPENDIX C

'NATIONAL' COACHES IN ROYAL BLUE LIVERY

Repainting of Bedford OB National coaches from cream and green to cream and blue livery and seat reduction from 29 to 27 at dates given below for use as duplicates on Royal Blue services

1953 *Repaint only*

587	HOD 132	6/53	590	HOD 135	6/53

1955 *Repaint and seat reduction*

580	HOD 120	5/55	1416	LTA 755	5/55
596	HOD 75	11/55	1417	LTA 756	4/55
597	HOD 76	11/55	1418	LTA 757	5/55
598	HOD 77	11/55	1419	LTA 758	4/55
1403	HOD 82	3/55	1431	LTA 907	4/55
1406	LTA 745	12/55	1432	LTA 908	4/55
1407	LTA 746	12/55	1445	LTA 921	4/55
1408	LTA 747	3/55	1446	LTA 922	5/55
1409	LTA 748	3/55	1447	LTA 923	5/55
1411	LTA 750	4/55	1448	LTA 924	3/55
1412	LTA 751	4/55	1449	LTA 925	3/55
1413	LTA 752	4/55	1450	LTA 926	3/55
1415	LTA 754	3/55			

Seat reduction only

587	HOD 132	5/55	590	HOD 135	5/55

1956 *Repaint and seat reduction*

594	HOD	73	1/56	1430	LTA	906	2/56
595	HOD	74	2/56	1440	LTA	916	1/56
1414	LTA	753	1/56	1441	LTA	917	1/56
1420	LTA	759	1/56	1442	LTA	918	2/56
1427	LTA	903	2/56	1443	LTA	919	2/56
1428	LTA	904	2/56	1444	LTA	920	1/56
1429	LTA	905	2/56				

1957 *Repaint and seat reduction*

581	HOD	121	3/57	1401	HOD	80	4/57
582	HOD	122	3/57	1402	HOD	81	5/57
583	HOD	128	2/57	1404	HOD	83	4/57
584	HOD	129	4/57	1405	KUO	726	5/57
585	HOD	130	4/57	1410	LTA	749	4/57
586	HOD	131	4/57	1433	LTA	909	4/57
588	HOD	133	3/57	1434	LTA	910	2/57
589	HOD	134	5/57	1435	LTA	911	3/57
591	HOD	70	3/57	1436	LTA	912	4/57
592	HOD	71	3/57	1437	LTA	913	3/57
593	HOD	72	5/57	1438	LTA	914	2/57
599	HOD	78	4/57	1439	LTA	915	3/57
1400	HOD	79	5/57				

1963

In 1963, 14 coaches new to the Western and Southern National coach fleets were
delivered temporarily for use as Royal Blue vehicles. The perspex fleetname read
'Royal Blue' until the delivery of 14 RELH6G coaches in 1964 when the respective
Western and Southern National perspex fleetnames were substituted. The vehicles
were as follows :

Western National					*Southern National*			
1398	736 MDV	Bristol	MW6G		1408	757 MDV	Bristol	MW6G
1399	737 MDV	,,	,,		1409	758 MDV	,,	,,
1400	738 MDV	,,	,,		1410	759 MDV	,,	,,
1401	739 MDV	,,	,,		1411	760 MDV	,,	,,
1402	740 MDV	,,	,,					
1403	741 MDV	,,	,,					
1404	742 MDV	,,	,,					
1405	743 MDV	,,	,,					
1406	744 MDV	,,	,,					
1407	745 MDV	,,	,,					

NOTE : (a) These 14 coaches were the first new Western and Southern National coaches
to have the same livery as Royal Blue coaches.
(b) All the above have air suspension and bodywork of 31 ft in length. They
are identical to cars 2271-80.

APPENDIX D

ROYAL BLUE VEHICLES WHICH OPERATED ON PRODUCER GAS

Car	Regn	Make & Type	Date Degassed	Engine Type	
WN 163	BTA 453	Bristol JJW	12/45		
SN 164	BTA 454	,, ,,	?		
WN 165	BTA 455	,, ,,	?		
SN 166	BTA 456	,, ,,	?		
WN 167	BTA 457	,, ,,	12/45		
SN 168	BTA 458	,, ,,	?	Bristol	
WN 169	BTA 459	,, ,,	?	'JW'	
SN 170	BTA 460	,, ,,	3/44	6 Cyl	
WN 173	ATT 923	,, ,,	2/45	41 hp	
WN 174	ATT 924	,, ,,	2/45	Petrol	
WN 177	ATT 927	,, ,,	11/45		
WN 178	ATT 928	,, ,,	11/45		
WN 179	ATT 929	,, ,,	11/45		
SN 184	ATT 934	,, ,,	2/45		
SN 187	ATT 937	,, ,,	2/45		
SN 188	ATT 938	,, ,,	11/45		
SN 190	ATT 940	,, ,,	11/45		
WN 2863	UU 1566	Leyland TS2	11/44	Leyland	Petrol
WN 2864	DR 5255	,, ,,	7/45	,,	,,
WN 3568*	DV 4890	,, ,,	11/44	,,	,,
WN 3569*	DV 4891	,, ,,	?	,,	,,
WN 3570*	DV 4889	,, ,,	1/45	,,	..
WN 3571*	DV 4925	,, ,,	3/45	,,	,,
WN 3572*	DV 5475	,, ,,	?	,,	,,
WN 3573*	DV 5476	,, ,,	11/44	,,	,,

NOTE: (a) Of the batch 163–90, nos 184 and 188 were delivered new as Southern National coaches and passed to the Royal Blue fleet in August 1937.

(b) Tilling type 2T2 Producer Gas trailers were used and hoppers were towed behind the vehicles.

It is not necessarily true to say that all the above were operating on gas at the same time. The seven whose dates of degassing are not known could well have been earlier conversions. The maximum mileage possible on gas with one engine is only about 50,000 as, after this, damage to the valves and combustion chamber ruins the unit.

(c) * Used on troop movements during the early part of the war; subsequently converted to gas producer operation and used on stage carriage bus services until returned to Royal Blue fleet in mid-1947.

APPENDIX E

ALLOCATION OF ROYAL BLUE VEHICLES
SUMMER 1969

Bournemouth	33
London	17
Portsmouth	11
Exeter	1
	62

Penzance	3
Camborne	2
St Austell	1
Helston	2
	8

Plymouth	7
Kingsbridge	1
Callington	1
Totnes	1
	10

Weymouth	2

Taunton	2
Bridgwater	1
	3

Bude	2
Ilfracombe	3
Bideford	1
Delabole	1
	7

TOTAL: 92
SPARES: 16 Royal Blue
8 for Associated Motorways
116 VEHICLES

Fleet No	Original direction indicators	Flashers fitted
WN 1279	Semaphore at extreme front below waist level	1/64
WN 1280		12/63
WN 1281		3/64
WN 1282		4/64
WN 1283		7/63
WN 1284		6/63
WN 1285		4/64
SN 1286		4/64
SN 1287		12/63
SN 1288		3/63
SN 1289		4/63
SN 1290		10/63
SN 1291		4/64
SN 1292		1/64
SN 1293	Semaphore on first straight pillar below waist level	1/63
SN 1294		4/63
SN 1295		2/64
SN 1296		4/63
SN 1297		4/64
SN 1298		4/64
SN 1299		4/64
WN 2200		3/63
WN 2201		3/64
WN 2202		4/63
WN 2203	Flashing on first straight pillar below waist level	
WN 2204		
WN 2205		
WN 2206		
WN 2207		
WN 2208		
SN 2209		
SN 2210		Not applicable
SN 2211		
SN 2212		
SN 2213		
SN 2214		

36 COACHES   WN = Western National
                                SN = Southern National

ROYAL BLUE BRISTOL LS6G VEHICLES

Characteristics of body design				
Curved front quarter lights	Incorporated roof luggage containers	Wind-down windscreens	ROYAL BLUE COACH SERVICE (see p 183)	To WN 3/62
Two full width screens at front	No roof luggage containers	Hinged windscreens	Glass roof quarter lights	

NOTES:

(a) The LS type coach body has no frontal radiator grill.

(b) The 'Royal Blue' motif was affixed approximately central between the bottom apron and the 'Bristol' fins on cars 1279–99 and 2200–2202. On cars 2203–14 the motif was raised to within an inch of the 'Bristol' fins, possibly anticipating the grill situated on MW coaches.

(c) All LS coach bodies have a polished chrome strip running at floor level on the outside of the body between the wheel arches.

(d) On the coaches with roof luggage containers a ladder rises centrally up the back of the body. The steps are hinged so that when not in use, they fit flush with the body. Chrome hand rails aid the driver when he climbs the ladder to load cases. Two doors hinged on their outer edges give access to the boot, which is of quite sizeable proportion, the central ladder dividing them on their locking sides.

(e) The passenger door, which incorporates a sighting window, opens outwards, being hinged at the front edge.

(f) On all LS coaches in the Royal Blue fleet, the roof level destination box in the front dome is shaped as shown on p 182.

N

APPENDIX G

ROYAL BLUE BRISTOL MW VEHICLES

(a) Coaches 2215–41 have flashing indicators mounted above waist level on the wide portion of the first straight pillar.

(b) Coaches 2242–69 have flashing indicators mounted below waist level on the first straight pillar.

They have Hopper type window vents as distinct from horizontal sliding ones on previous coaches.

Like all previous coaches, they have three transparent roof lights. However, unlike previous batches, the centre roof light is non-opening type and is fitted flush with the body.

(c) As all MW passenger doors open inwards, there is a slot provided for the step which would otherwise foul the swing of the door as it opens.

(d) Like the last batch of LSs, the MW boot lid is hinged at the top edge.

(e) Coaches 2270–80 are described in Chapter 10.

APPENDIX H

RAILWAY LINES AND STATIONS ADJACENT TO ROYAL BLUE ROUTES, CLOSED TO PASSENGER TRAFFIC SINCE THE SECOND WORLD WAR

1951 Burnham-on-Sea station
Little Somerford–Malmesbury
1952 Weymouth–Portland–Easton
Bulford Camp branch
Bisley Camp branch
Weymouth–Abbotsbury
1953 Swindon–Highworth
Fareham–Gosport
1955 Meon Valley line: Alton–Fareham
Ludgershall–Tidworth
1956 Yelverton–Princetown
1957 Bentley–Bordon
1958 Teign Valley line: Exeter–Heathfield
Totnes–Ashburton†
1959 Newton Abbot–Moretonhampstead
Local stations between Plympton & S Brent
Bristol–Frome
1960 Carn Brea station
Newbury–Winchester
1961 Local stations on Bristol–Swindon main line
Swindon–Savernake–Andover
Norton Fitzwarren station
1962 Local stations between Langport & Castle Cary
Launceston–Plymouth
Taunton–Chard
Gwinear Road–Helston
1963 Brent–Kingsbridge
Culm Valley line: Tiverton Junc–Hemyock
Exe Valley line: Exeter–Dulverton
Chacewater–Newquay
Churston Ferrers–Brixham
Yatton–Cheddar–Wells–Witham
Havant–Hayling Island
Oakley station
1964 Local stations between Swindon and Reading
Tiverton–Tiverton Junc
Local stations on the Exeter–Taunton main line
Local stations on the Plymouth–Penzance main line
Local stations on the Bristol–Taunton main line
S Brent station
Langport–Yeovil
Local stations between Langport and Taunton

Hurstbourne station
Knowle Halt
Salisbury–Fordingbridge–West Moors
Broadstone–Wimborne–Ringwood–Brockenhurst*
Andover–Stockbridge–Romsey
1965 Lostwithiel–Fowey
Torrington–Halwill Junc
Chippenham–Calne
Axminster–Lyme Regis
Local stations between Bristol and Swindon via Bath
Boscombe station
Bournemouth West station
1966 Taunton–Barnstaple
Barnstaple–Torrington
Local stations between Savernake and Frome
Local stations between Exeter and Salisbury
Somerset & Dorset line
Patney & Chirton–Semington
Chippenham–Staverton
Callington–Gunnislake
Seaton–Seaton Junc
Local stations between Bristol and Weymouth
Okehampton–Bude
Halwill Junc–Wadebridge
Yatton–Clevedon
Totton–Fawley
Broadstone station & Creekmoor halt
Wilton South station
Northam–Southampton terminus
1967 Sidmouth–Sidmouth Junc
Tipton St John–Exmouth
Padstow–Bodmin Road
1968 Yeovil–Yeovil Junc
Okehampton–Tavistock–Bere-Alston

* This was indeed a sad occasion, as the Broadstone–Brockenhurst line included Holmsley Road station, which had given birth to Royal Blue in 1880 (see Chapter 1). The wheel had turned full circle.

† Reopened Summer 1969 as a 'rail enthusiasts' line' with steam traction.

INDEX

References to illustrations are indicated by heavy type